D0454153

CONTENTS

The representation on the maps of a road, or footpath is no evidence of the existence of a Right of Way.

Every possible care has been taken to ensure that the information given in this Atlas is accurate and whilst the publishers would be grateful to learn of any errors, they regret they can accept no responsibility for any expense or loss thereby caused.

The maps in this Atlas are based upon the Ordnance Survey Maps with the sanction of the Controller of Her Majesty's Stationery Office. Crown Copyright Reserved.

An A to Z publication   ISBN 0 85039 139 3

SCALE
1:7,040
9 inches to 1 Mile

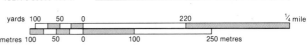

yards 100   50   0   220   ¼ mile

metres 100   50   0   100   250 metres

REFERENCE

Motorway	
Dual Carriageway	
'A' Road	A41
'B' Road	B106
One Way Street	
Railway Station Entrances	British Rail / Docklands Light Railway DLR / Underground
District & Borough Boundary	
Postal District Boundary By arrangement with the Post Office	E.C.1.
Building open to the Public	
Fire Station	■
Hospital	
House Numbers 'A' & 'B' Roads only	2 45
Information Centre	🛈
Map Continuation	30
Place of Interest	
Police Station	▲
Post Office	★
Toilet	▽
Disabled Toilet (National Key Scheme)	♿

Geographers' A-Z Map Co. Ltd.

Head Office : Fairfield Road, Borough Green,
Sevenoaks, Kent. TN15 8PP
Telephone 0732-781000

Showrooms :
44 Gray's Inn Road, London, WC1X 8LR
Telephone 071-242 9246

Edition 4   1990
Edition 4B (part revision) 1992

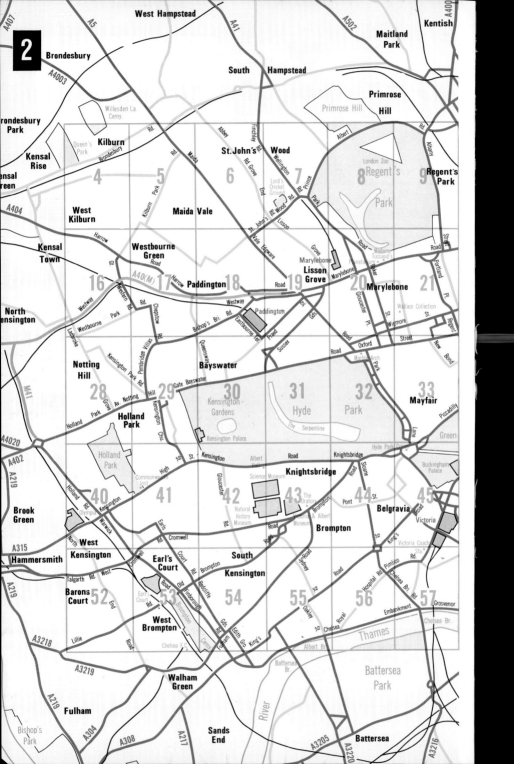

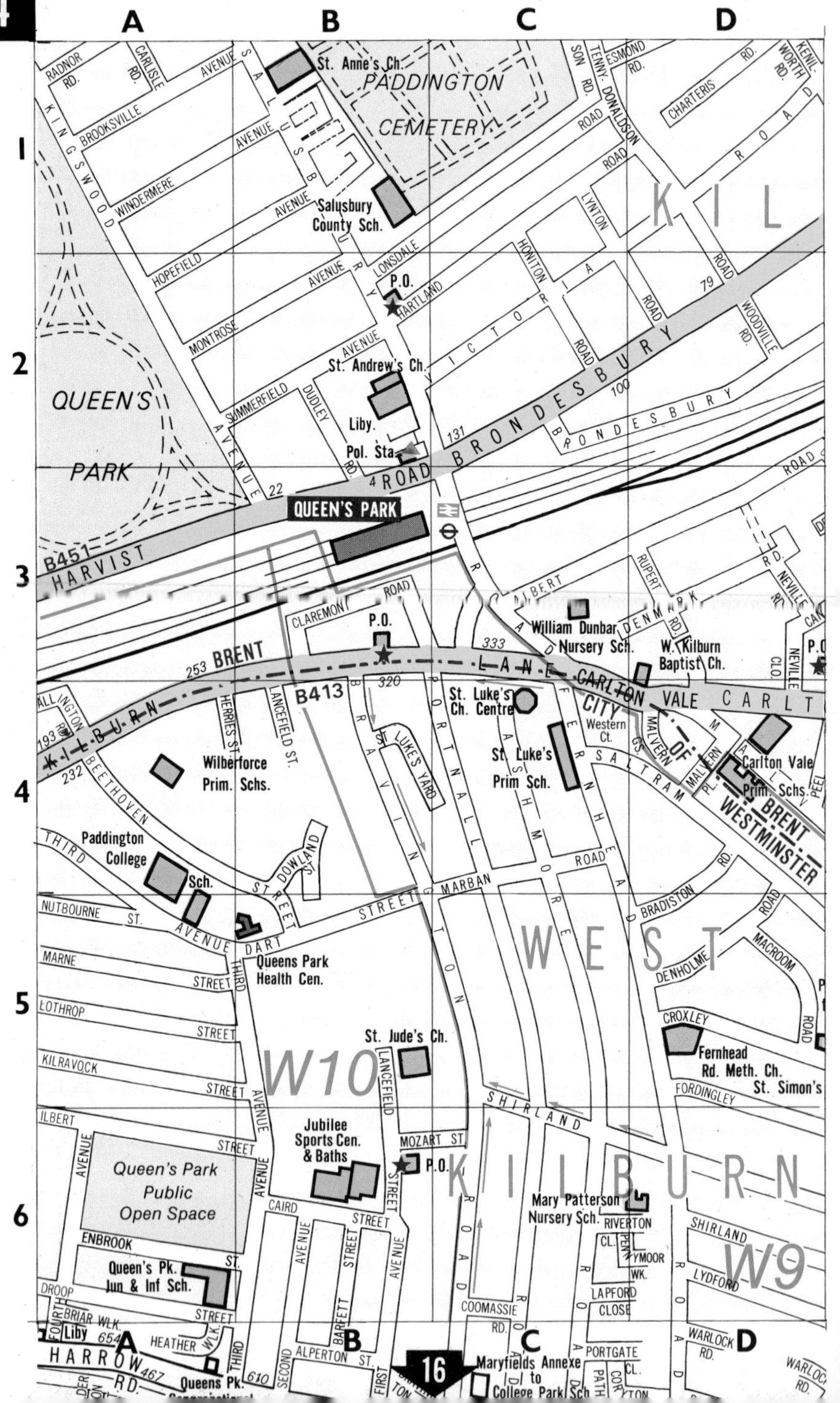

A B C D

1

RADNOR RD.
CARLISLE RD.
AVENUE
St. Anne's Ch.
PADDINGTON
CEMETERY
BROOKSVILLE
KINGSWOOD
WINDERMERE
AVENUE
AVENUE
Salusbury
County Sch.
SON RD.
TENNY.
ESMOND RD.
DONALDSON ROAD
CHARTERIS RD.
KENT.
WORTH RD.
ROAD
KIL
HOPEFIELD
AVENUE
LONSDALE
P.O.
HARTLAND
LYNTON ROAD
HONITON RD.
VICTORIA ROAD
ROAD
WOODVILLE RD.
79

2

QUEEN'S
PARK
MONTROSE
AVENUE
SUMMERFIELD
AVENUE
DUDLEY
AVENUE
St. Andrew's Ch.
Liby.
Pol. Sta.
ROAD
22
131
BRONDESBURY
4
100
BRONDESBURY
ROAD

3

B451
HARVIST
QUEEN'S PARK
CLAREMONT
ROAD
P.O.
BRENT
253
333
320
L A N E
ALBERT RD.
RUPERT RD.
William Dunbar
Nursery Sch.
DENMARK RD.
W. Kilburn
Baptist Ch.
CARLTON VALE
NEVILLE RD.
P.O.
CLO.
NEVILLE
CARLT
CAN.

4

KILBURN
193
232
BEETHOVEN
HERRIES ST.
LANEFIELD ST.
B413
Wilberforce
Prim. Schs.
St. LUKE'S YARD
PORTNALL
St. Luke's
Ch. Centre
Western Ct.
St. Luke's
Prim. Sch.
FERNHEAD
SALTRAM
MALVERN PL.
MALVERN
Carlton Vale
Prim. Schs.
BRENT
WESTMINSTER
PEEL
CITY OF

5

THIRD
Paddington
College
Sch.
DART STREET
DOWLAND STREET
NUTBOURNE ST.
MARNE
STREET
AVENUE
MARBAN STREET
Queens Park
Health Cen.
W10
LOTHROP
STREET
KILRAVOCK
STREET
St. Jude's Ch.
LANEFIELD
SHIRLAND
WEST
ROAD
BRADISTON
DENHOLME ROAD
MACROOM RD.
CROXLEY
Fernhead
Rd. Meth. Ch.
St. Simon's
FORDINGLEY

6

ILBERT
AVENUE
STREET
Queen's Park
Public
Open Space
CAIRD STREET
AVENUE
BARRETT STREET
AVENUE
Jubilee
Sports Cen.
& Baths
MOZART ST.
P.O.
ROAD
SHIRLAND
KILBURN
Mary Patterson
Nursery Sch.
RIVERTON
CL.
PENRY. MOOR WK.
LAPFORD
CLOSE
SHIRLAND RD.
W9
LYDFORD
WARLOCK RD.

ENBROOK
DROOP
Queen's Pk.
Jun & Inf Sch.
BRIAR WLK.
654
Liby.
HEATHER WLK.
THIRD
SECOND
ALPERTON
FIRST
FIXTON ST.
COOMASSIE RD.
PORTGATE
COR. PATH
16
Maryfields Annexe
to
College Park Sch
HARROW RD.
467
Queens Pk.
Congregational
610
WARLOCK

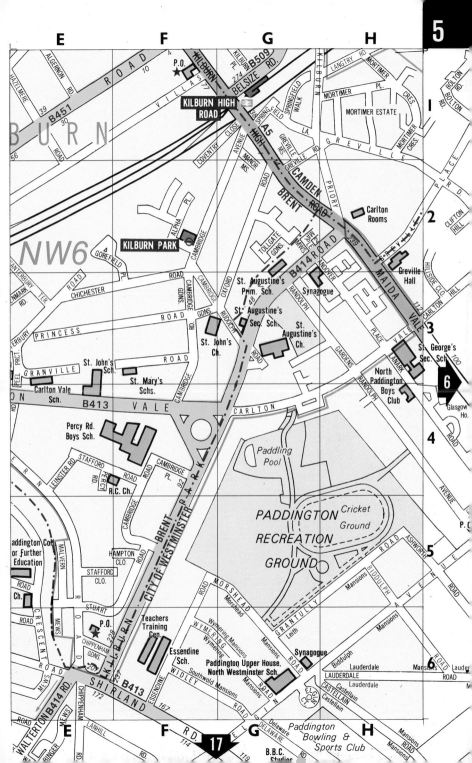

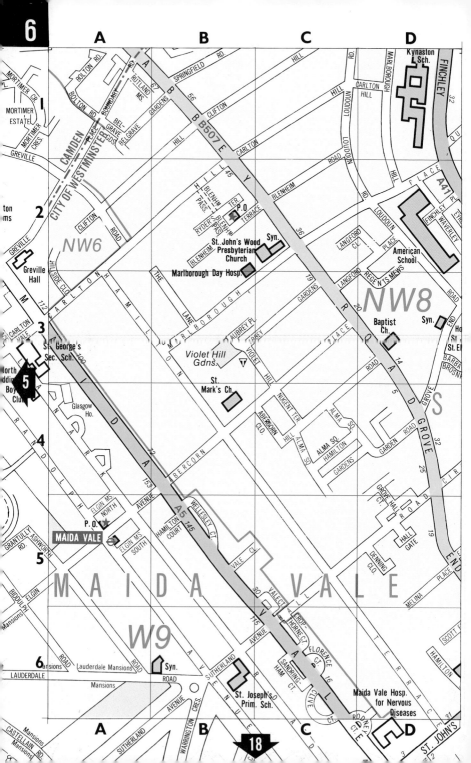

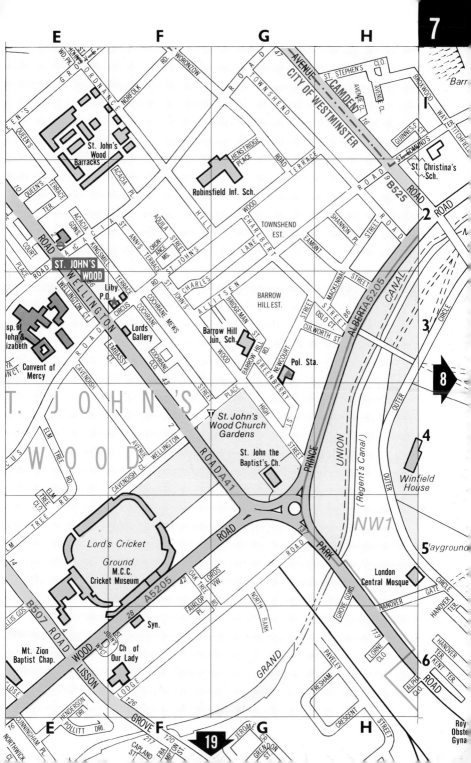

A   B   C   D

PRIMROSE HILL

Reservoir

Barrow Hill

CAMDEN

ALBERT ROAD

NW8

CITY OF WESTMINSTER

A5205

ALBERT

Snowdon
Aviary

Main
Entrance

Refreshment
Roo

London Zoo

NW1

St.
Christina's
Sch.

Prince
Regent Court

Primrose Hill
Bri

(Regent's Canal)

Running Track

Macclesfield
Bri

Cricket Ground

7

R E G E N

Refreshments

Winfield
House

P A R K

Playground

London
Central Mosque

Children's
Boating Pond

Open Air
Theatre

QUEEN MARY

HANOVER   GATE

HANOVER   TERRACE

HANOVER
TER   MEWS

KENT   TER

GARDENS

La

PARK   CLO

LORNE   CLO

KENT   TER

Boating Lake

Bandstand

ALPHA   CLO

RD.   A41

SUSSEX   PASSAGE

A   B   C   D

Royal Coll. of
Obstetricians &
Gynaecologists
P.O.

20

Regent's College

YORK   BRIDGE

PAVELEY
ST

AVENUE   RD.

PRINCE

TOWNSHEND   RD

GUINNESS

BROXWOOD   WAY

WELLS

ST. EDMUND'S

CLO

DRUMMOND

ST. JAMES'S
MEWS

TITCHFIELD

ST. JAMES'S TER

OUTER   CIRCLE

OUTER   CIRCLE

INNER   CIRCLE

1

2

3

4

5

6

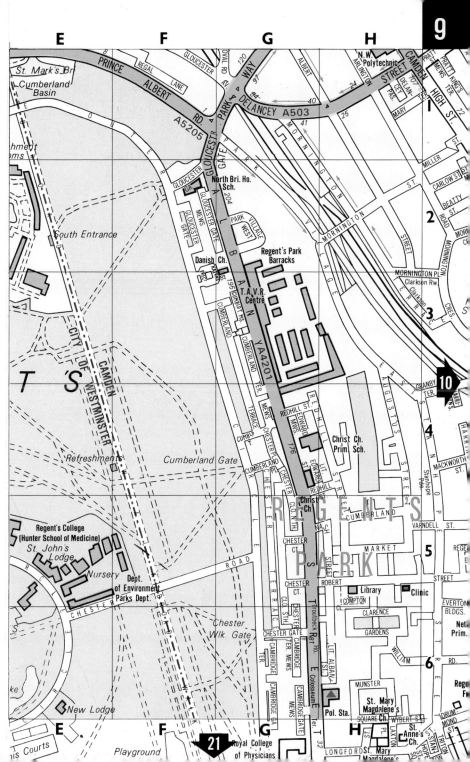

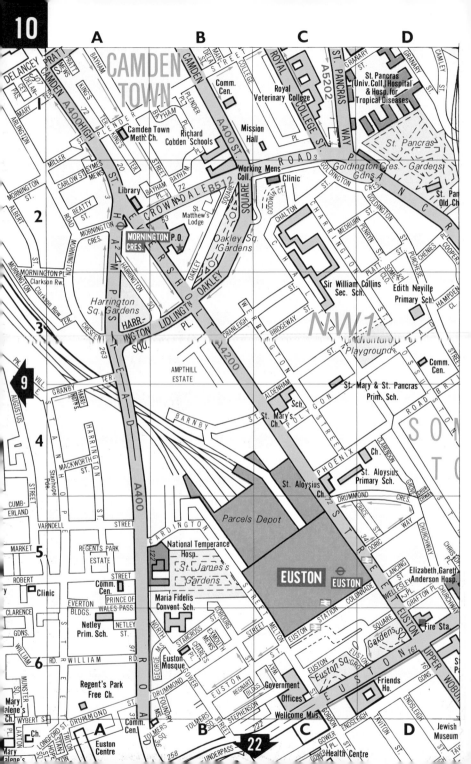

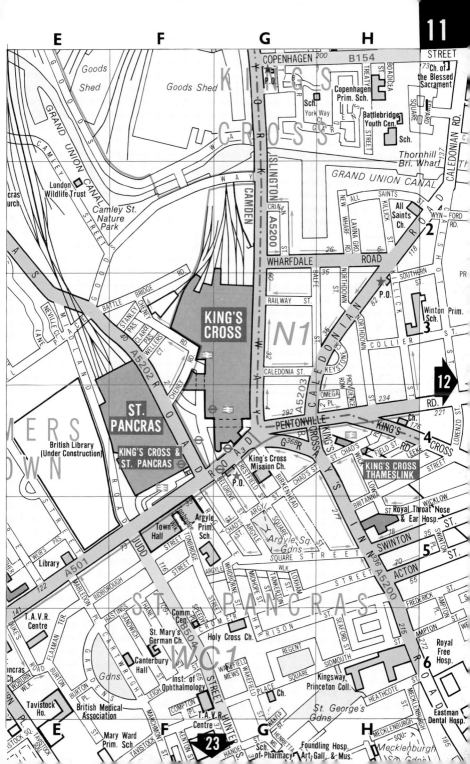

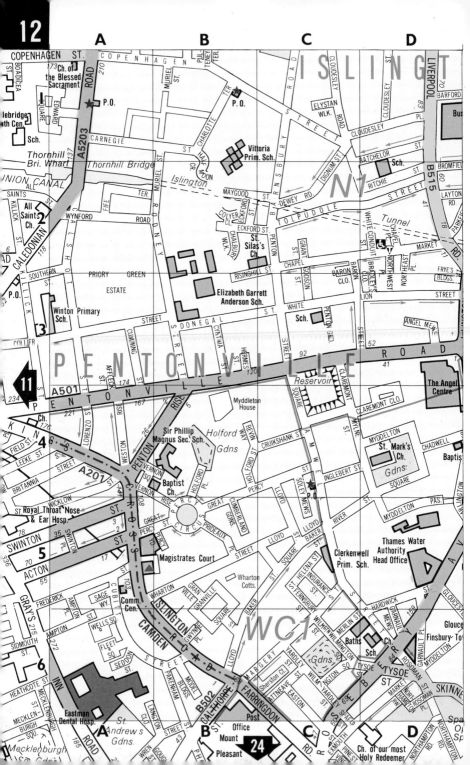

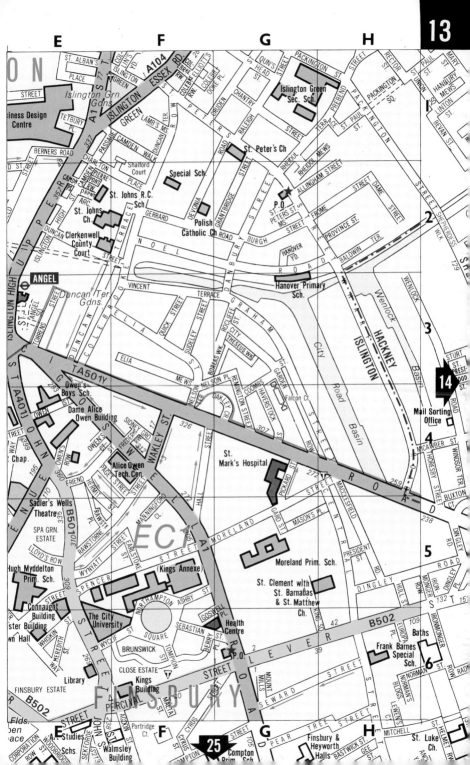

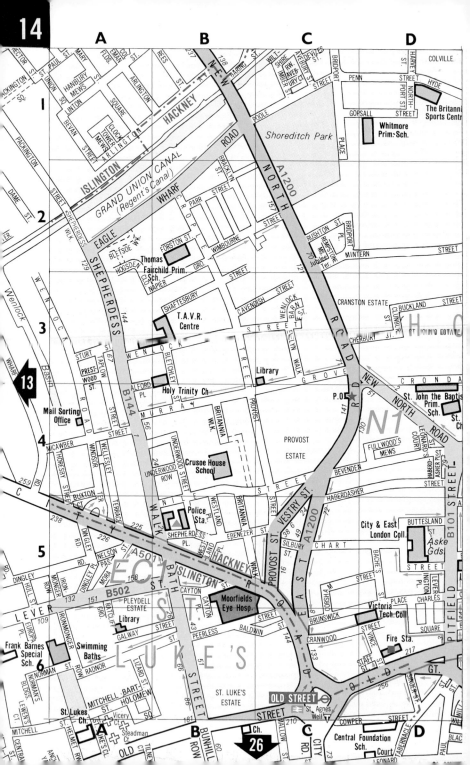

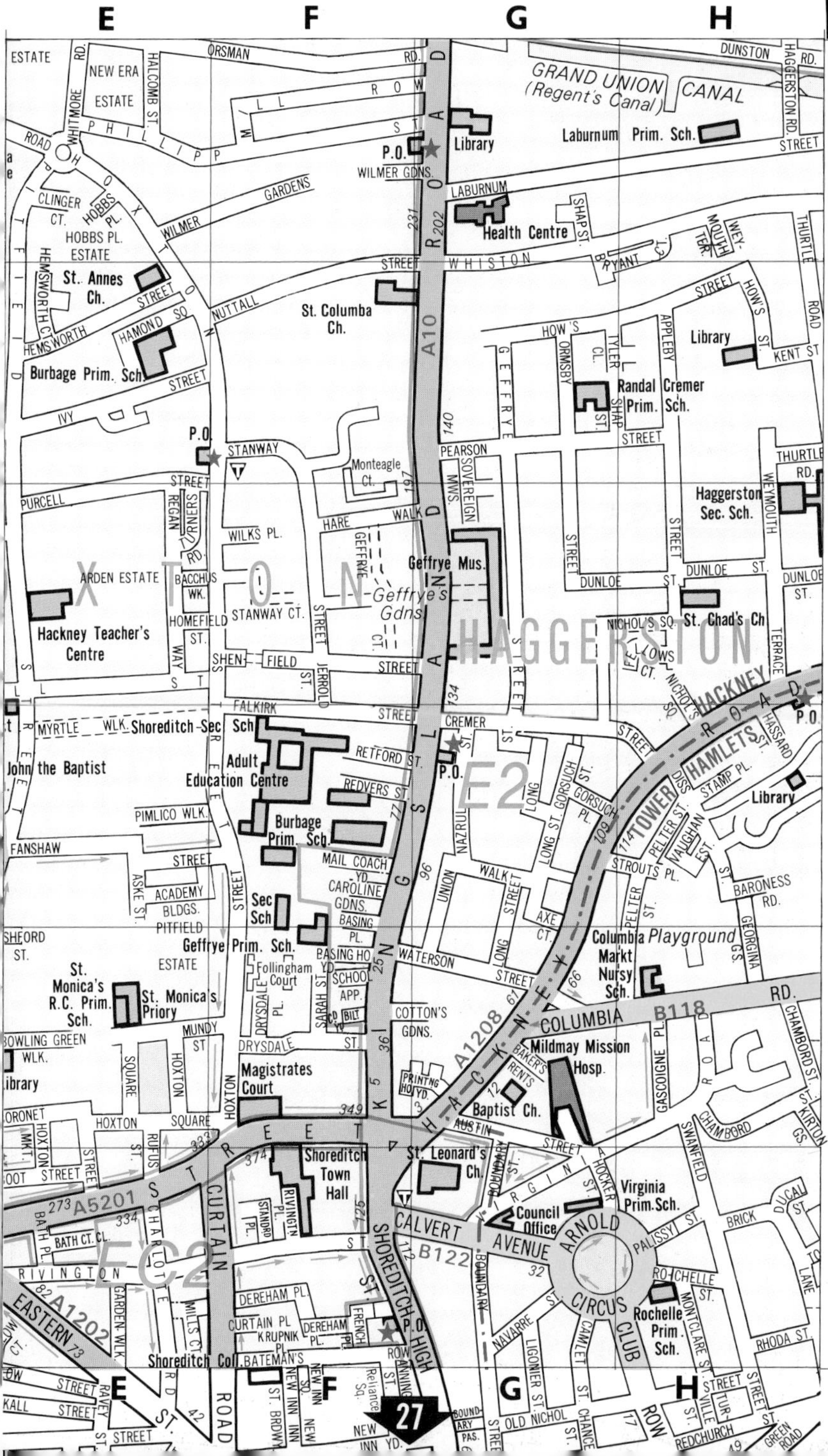

ESTATE

NEW ERA ESTATE

ORSMAN ROW RD.

DUNSTON STREET

GRAND UNION CANAL
(Regent's Canal)

WHITMORE

PHILLIPP

P.O. ★ Library

Laburnum Prim. Sch. I

CLINGER CT. HOBBS PL.

WILMER GARDENS

WILMER GDNS.

LABURNUM

WEY. MOUTH TERR.

THIRTLE

HOBBS PL. ESTATE

STREET WHISTON STREET

Health Centre

BRYANT

HOW'S ST.

ROAD

HEMSWORTH

St. Annes Ch.

STREET

St. Columba Ch.

APPLEBY

KENT ST.

2

HAMOND SQ. NUTTALL

HOW'S ORMSBY CL. TYLER

Library

Burbage Prim. Sch.

STREET

Randal Cremer Prim. Sch.

HON'S ST.

IVY

GEFFRYE SHAP ST.

STREET

THIRTLE RD.

PURCELL

P.O. ★ STANWAY

PEARSON

STREET

DUNLOE

Haggerston Sec. Sch.

WEYMOUTH

REGAN TURNER'S RD.

SOVEREIGN MWS.

DUNLOE ST.

ARDEN ESTATE

BACCHUS WK.

WILKS PL.

HARE

WALK

Geffrye Mus.

STREET

St. Chad's Ch

TERRACE

3

HOMEFIELD STANWAY CT.

Geffrye's Gdns

NICHOL'S SQ.

Hackney Teacher's Centre

SHEN FIELD

JERROLD

STREET

HAGGERSTON

NICHOLS

HACKNEY

FALKIRK

CREMER

John the Baptist

MYRTLE WLK. Shoreditch Sec Sch

RETFORD ST.

P.O. ★

E2

STAMP PL.

Library

TOWER HAMLETS

4

Adult Education Centre

REDVERS ST.

NAZRUL

HOUSGORSUCH

PELTER ST.

VAUGHAN EST.

BARONESS RD.

FANSHAW

PIMLICO WLK.

Burbage Prim. Sch.

MAIL COACH YD. CAROLINE GDNS.

UNION STREET

WALK

STROUTS PL.

PELTER ST.

GEORGINA

ACADEMY BLDGS.

SCHOOL APP.

AXE

GSS.

ASKE ST. PITFIELD

Sec Sch

BASING PL.

WATERSON STREET

CT.

Columbia Markt Nursy Sch.

Playground

RD.

SHEORD ST.

Geffrye Prim. Sch.

BASING HO

COTTON'S GDNS.

COLUMBIA

B118

CHAMBORD ST.

5

St. Monica's R.C. Prim. Sch.

St. Monica's Priory

ESTATE

FOLLINGHAM COURT

DRYSDALE PL.

A1208

BAKER'S RENTS

Mildmay Mission Hosp.

GASCOIGNE PL.

CHAMBORD

SIVILL

GSS.

BOWLING GREEN WLK.

MUNDY ST

DRYSDALE ST.

Magistrates Court

PRINTING HO YD

Baptist Ch.

SWANFIELD

DUGAL LANE

Library

HOXTON

SQUARE

HOXTON

RUFUS

AUSTIN

ROAD

BRICK LANE

6

CORONET

HOXTON ST.

S

Shoreditch Town Hall

RIVINGTON

St. Leonard's Ch.

VIRGIN

HOOKER

Virginia Prim. Sch.

PALISSY ST.

ROCHELLE ST.

FOOT STREET

A5201

BATH CT. CL.

CURTAIN

CALVERT AVENUE

Council Office

ARNOLD

Rochelle Prim. Sch.

MONTCLARE ST.

RHODA ST.

RIVINGTON

A1202

GARDEN WLK.

SHOREDITCH HIGH

B122

BOUNDARY

CIRCUS

CLUB

CAMLET

LIGONIER ST.

NAVARRE ST.

EASTERN

DEREHAM PL.

CURTAIN PL. DEREHAM PL.

FRENCH

RELIANCE

OLD NICHOL

CALVERT

TURN VILLE

GREEN ROAD

KALL STREET

KRUPNIK

Shoreditch Coll. BATEMAN'S

ROW

NEW INN

NEW INN

REDCHURCH

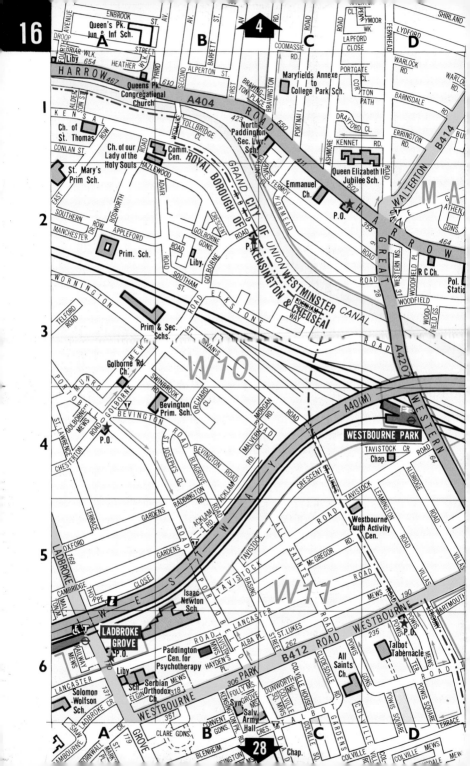

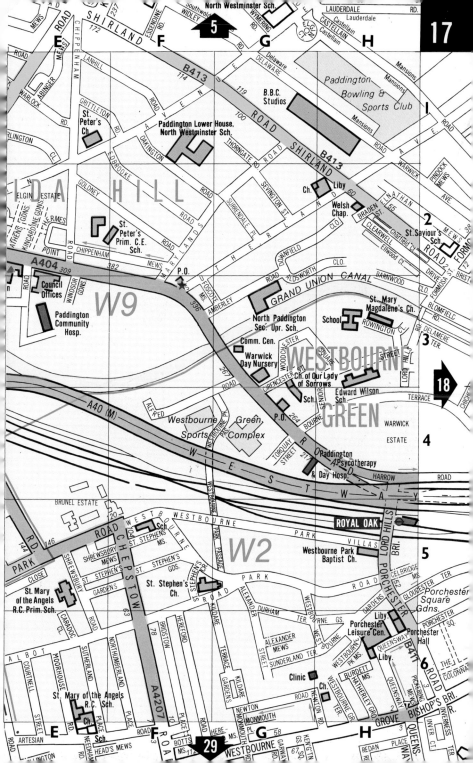

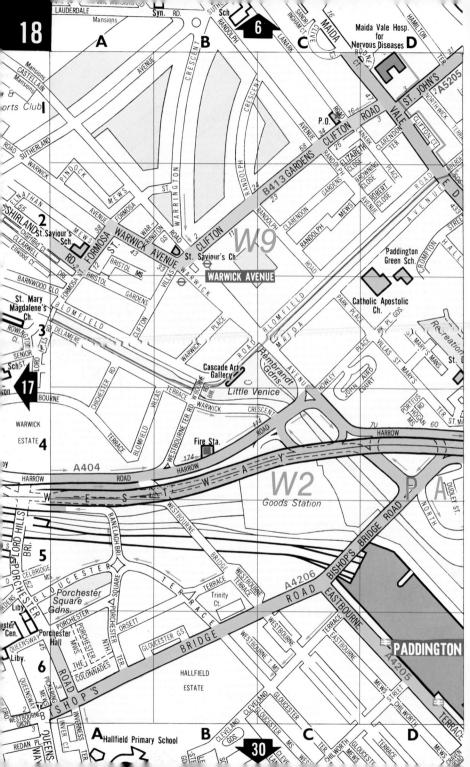

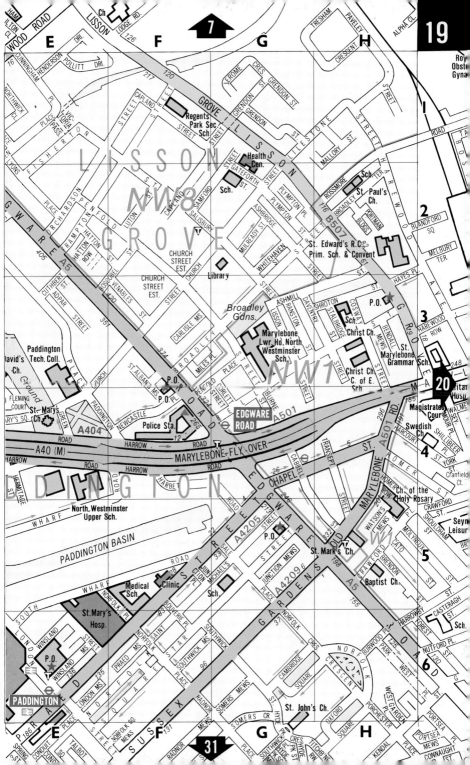

LISSON GROVE

NW8

LISSON GROVE

NW1

PADDINGTON

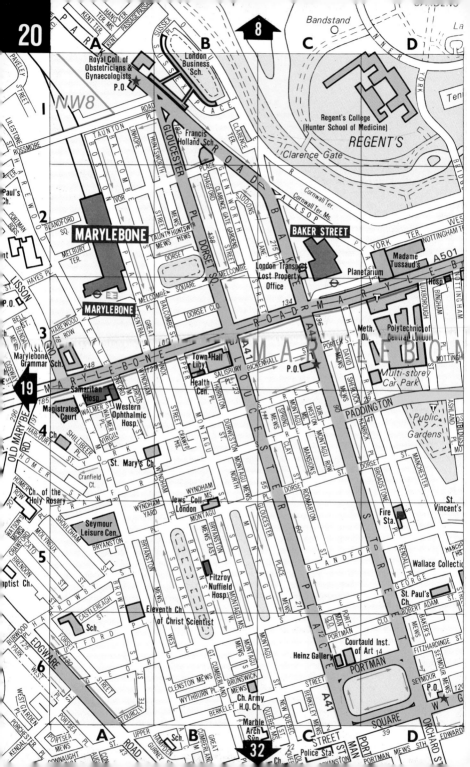

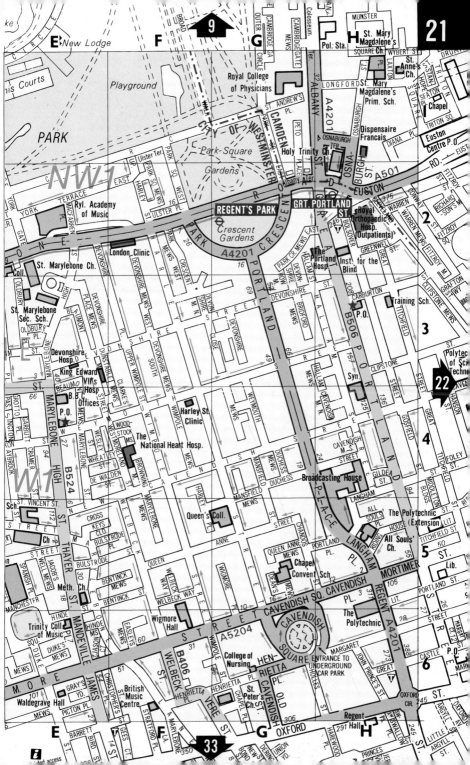

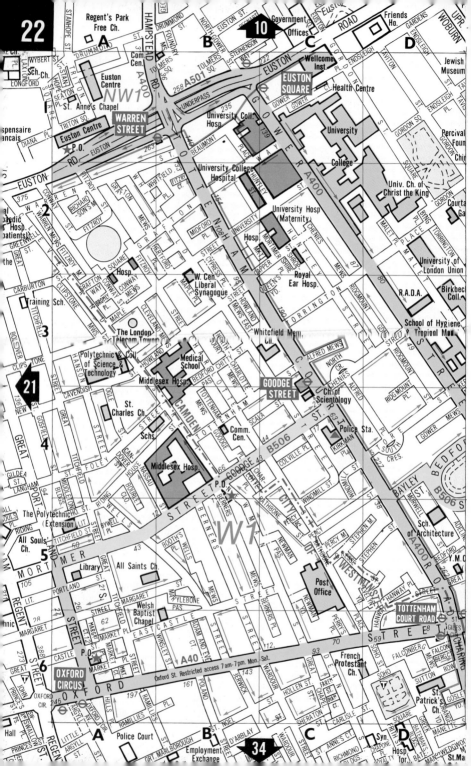

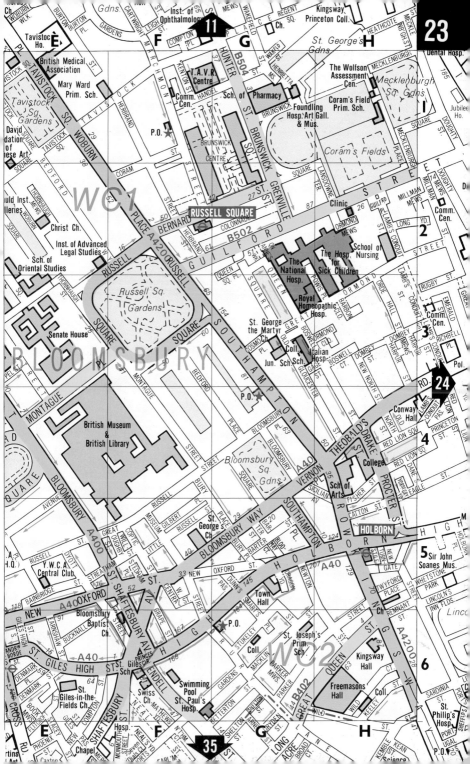

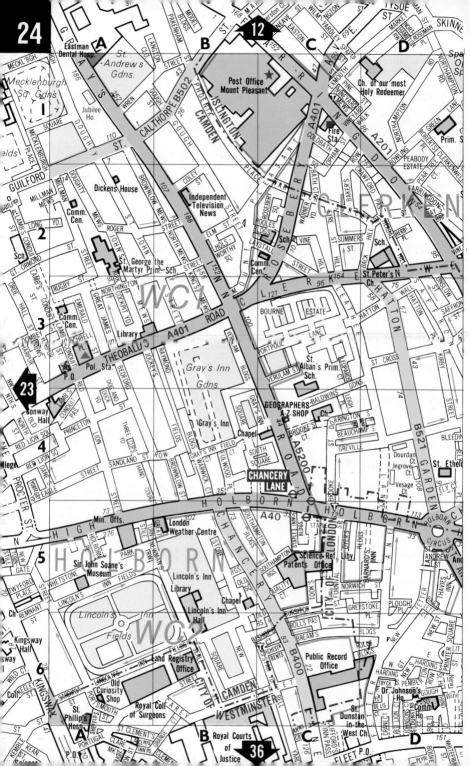

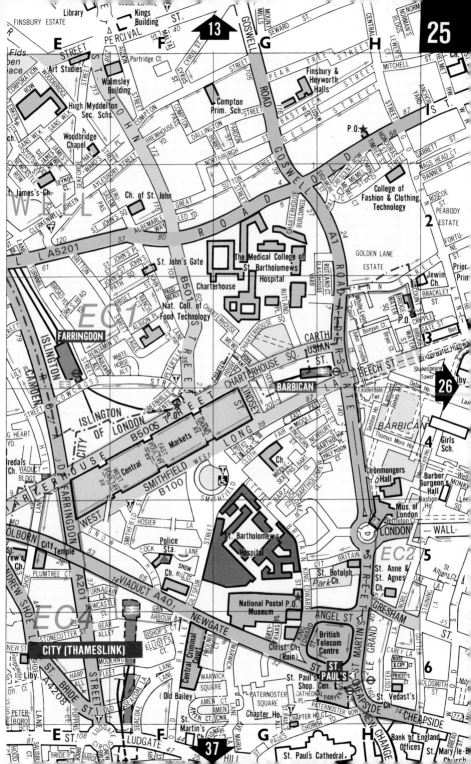

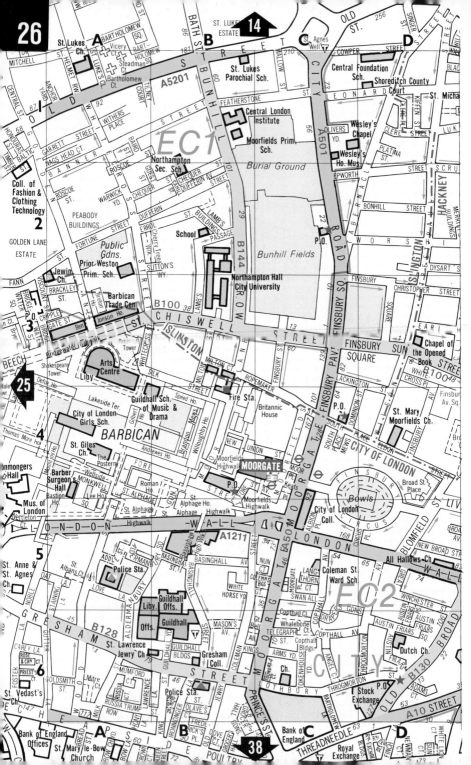

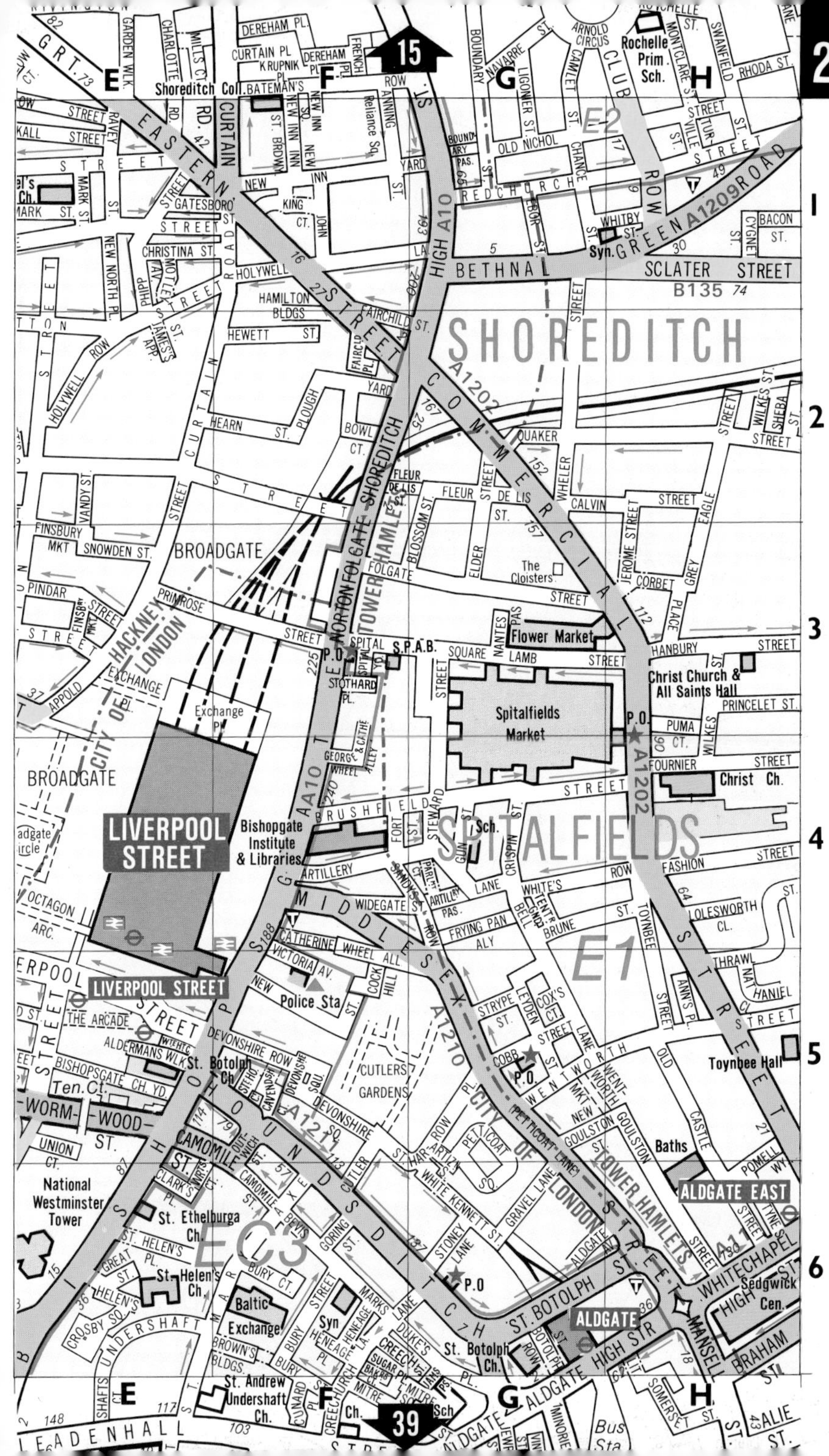

SHOREDITCH

SPITALFIELDS

BROADGATE

LIVERPOOL STREET

EC3

EC2

E1

CITY OF LONDON

TOWER HAMLETS

Spitalfields Market

Flower Market

Christ Church & All Saints Hall

Christ Ch.

Liverpool Street

Bishopsgate Institute & Libraries

National Westminster Tower

Police Sta

Toynbee Hall

Baths

Aldgate East

Aldgate

St. Botolph Ch.

St. Ethelburga

St. Helen's Ch.

Baltic Exchange

St. Andrew Undershaft Ch.

Rochelle Prim. Sch.

Shoreditch Coll.

The Cloisters

S.P.A.B.

P.O.

Syn

GREAT EASTERN STREET

COMMERCIAL STREET

SHOREDITCH HIGH STREET

BETHNAL GREEN ROAD

SCLATER STREET

REDCHURCH STREET

OLD NICHOL STREET

CURTAIN ROAD

NEW NORTH ROAD

CITY OF LONDON

BISHOPSGATE

MIDDLESEX STREET

HOUNDSDITCH

CAMOMILE STREET

WENTWORTH STREET

WHITECHAPEL HIGH STREET

ALDGATE HIGH STREET

LEADENHALL STREET

UNDERSHAFT

CROSBY

BRUSHFIELD STREET

FOLGATE STREET

FLEUR DE LIS STREET

QUAKER STREET

WHEELER STREET

BLOSSOM STREET

HANBURY STREET

PRINCELET STREET

FOURNIER STREET

FASHION STREET

WENTWORTH STREET

GOULSTON STREET

MANSELL STREET

A10

A1202

A1209

A1210

B135

15

39

E F G H I

1 2 3 4 5 6

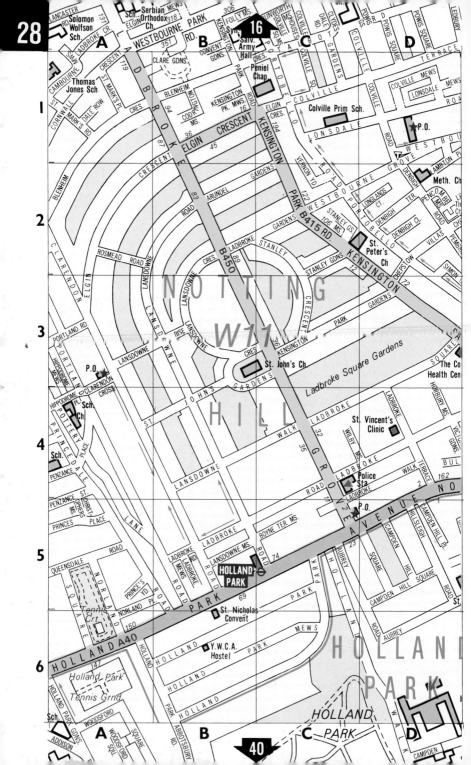

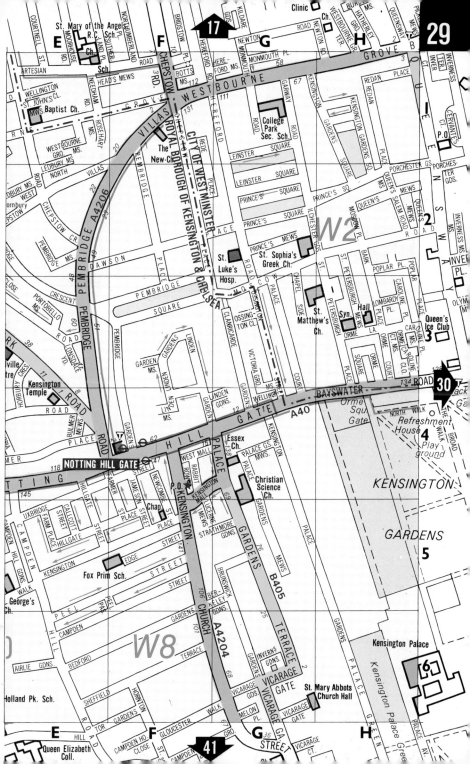

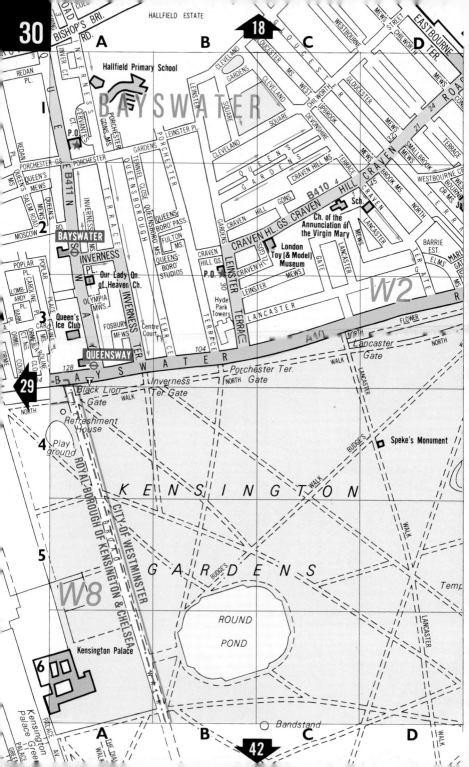

HALLFIELD ESTATE

18

A   B   C   D

BISHOP'S BRI.
ROAD

BAYSWATER

Hallfield Primary School

I

REDAN
PL.

P.O.

PORCHESTER GS.

REDAN
PL.

Queen's
Mews

QUEEN'S SALEM ROAD

MOSCOW
RD.

2 **BAYSWATER**

INVERNESS

Poplar
PL.

CAROLINE PLACE

LOMB-
ARDY
PL.

Our Lady Qn.
of Heaven Ch.

OLYMPIA
MWS.

CENTRE
COURT

3 Queen's
Ice Club

FOSBURY
MEWS

CARO
LINE
MS.

ORME
CT.

ORME
COURT

QUEENSWAY

29

NORTH

Black Lion
Gate

Refreshment
House

4 Play
ground

K E N S I N G T O N

5

W8

G A R D E N S

6 Kensington Palace

Kensington
Palace
Green

PALACE
AV.

THE DIAL WALK

ROYAL BOROUGH OF KENSINGTON & CHELSEA
CITY OF WESTMINSTER

CLEVELAND
GARDENS

CLEVELAND
SQUARE

CLEVELAND

PORCHESTER

QUEENSBOROUGH

TERRACE

QUEENS
BORO' PASS.

FULTON
MS.

QUEENS
BORO'
STUDIOS

CRAVEN
HILL GS.

LEINSTER PL.

LEINSTER

TENNIEL CLOSE

LEINSTER

P.O.
30

Hyde Park
Towers

104

CRAVEN HILL GS. CRAVEN HILL

B410 4

QUEEN'S
GARDENS

CRAVEN HILL GDNS.

CRAVEN HILL MS.

London
Toy (& Model)
Museum

LANCASTER

LEINSTER

LEINSTER

MEWS

LANCASTER

GLOUCES

WESTBOURNE

WESTBOURNE GS.

CHILWORTH

UPBROOK
MS.

DEVONSHIRE

CRAVEN

TERRACE

BROOK MS.

CRAVEN
TERRACE

Sch.

Ch. of the
Annunciation of
the Virgin Mary

GATE

W2

NORTH
WALK

Porchester Ter.
NORTH Gate

Inverness
Ter. Gate

WALK

BUDGE'S

WALK

ROUND
POND

BUDGE'S

WALK

Bandstand

MEWS STREET CHILWORTH

WESTBOURNE

GLOUCES

EASTBOURNE TER.

ROAD

24

32?

21

SMALLBROOK
MEWS

CRAVEN

TERRACE

NORTH

45

LANCASTER

TERRACE

GATE

WESTBOURNE CR.

NORTH WESTBOURNE CR. MS.

BAYSWATER JN

BARRIE
EST.

ELMS

BARRIE
EST.
MS.

MARL

FLOWER

NORTH

Lancaster
Gate

Speke's Monument

L A N C A S T E R

LANCASTER

Temp

42

29

128

34

BAYSWATER

INVERNESS

W A L K

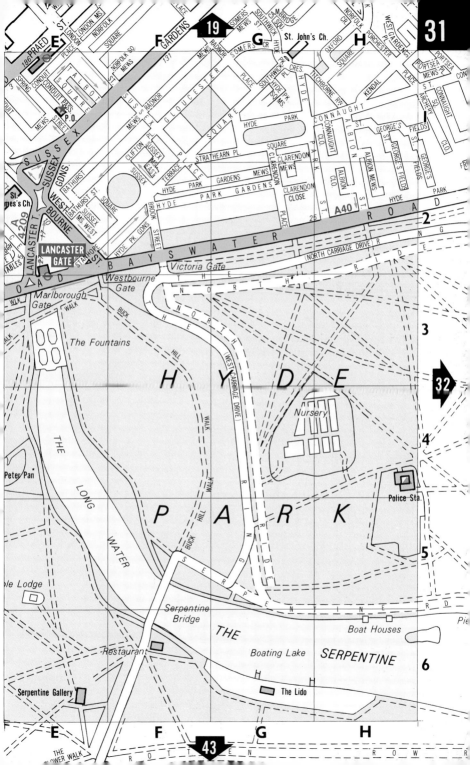

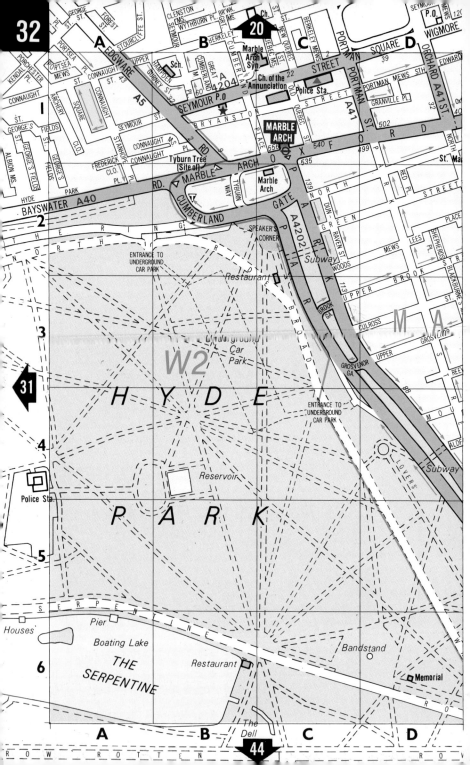

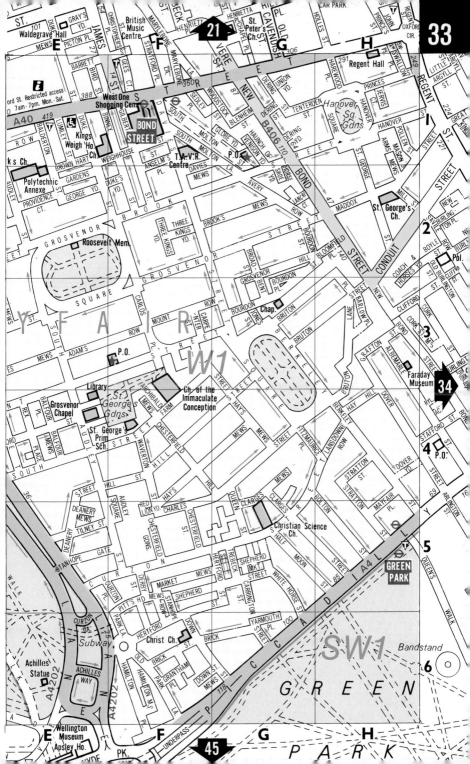

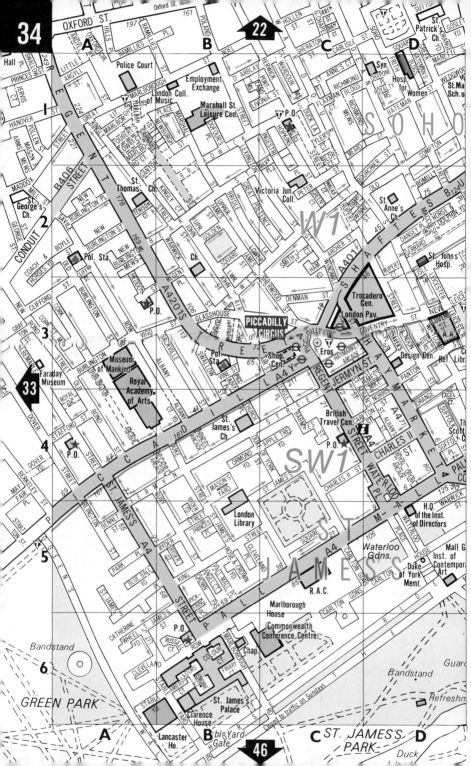

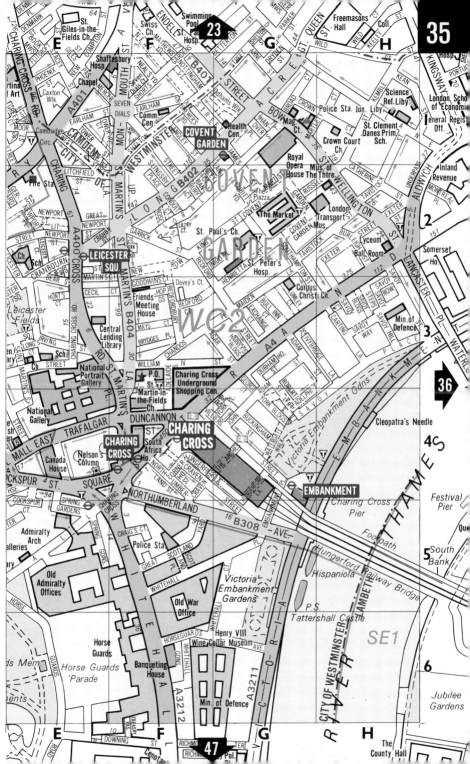

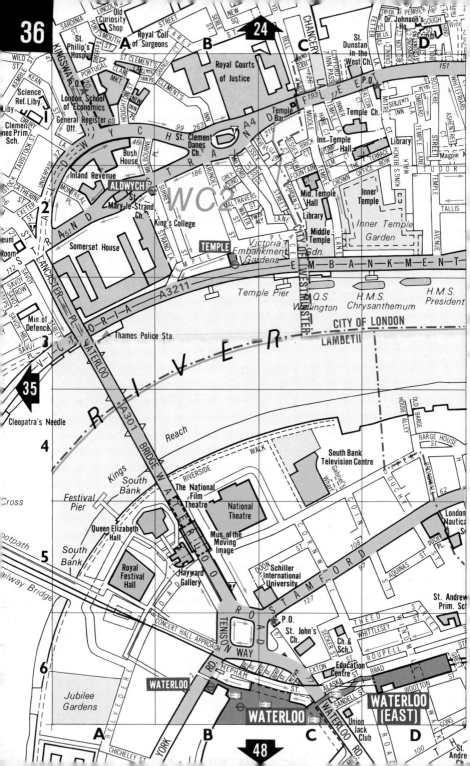

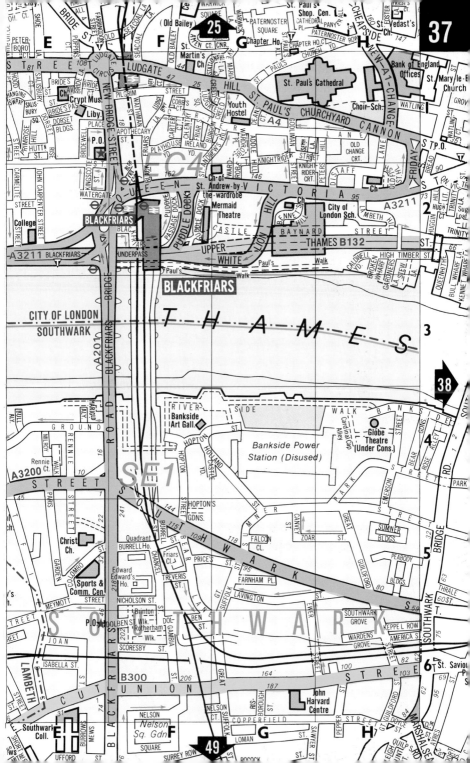

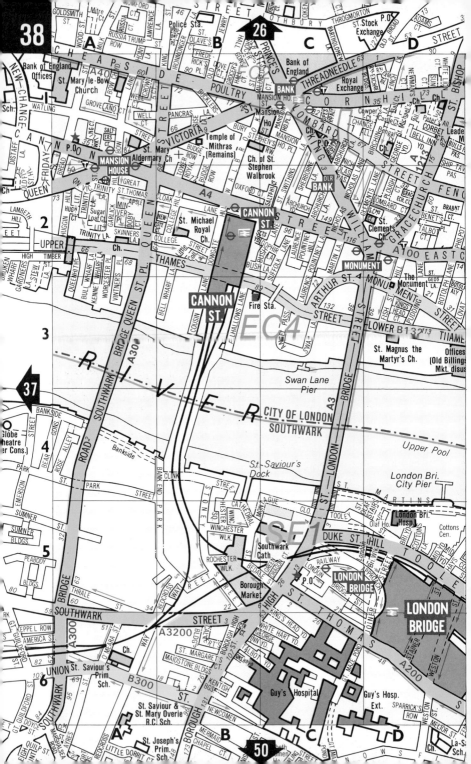

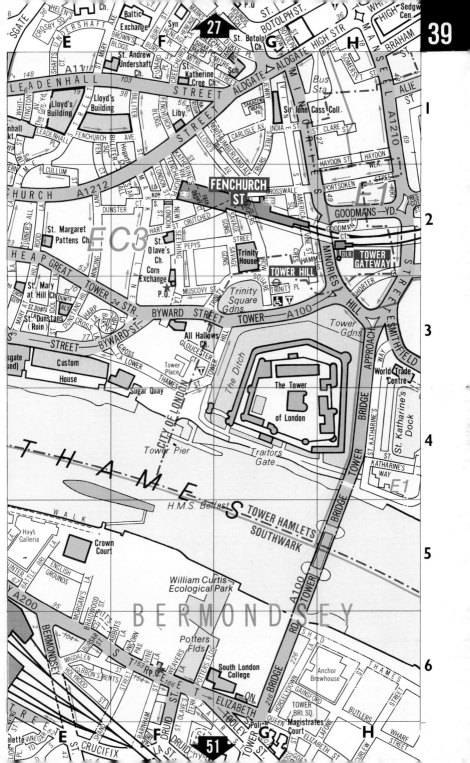

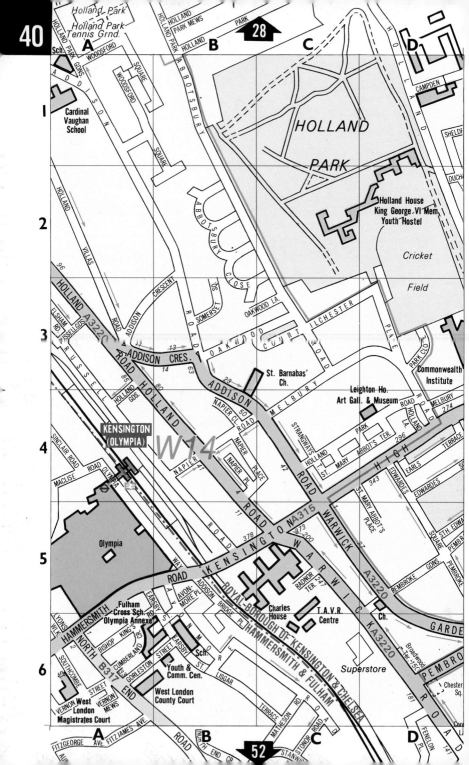

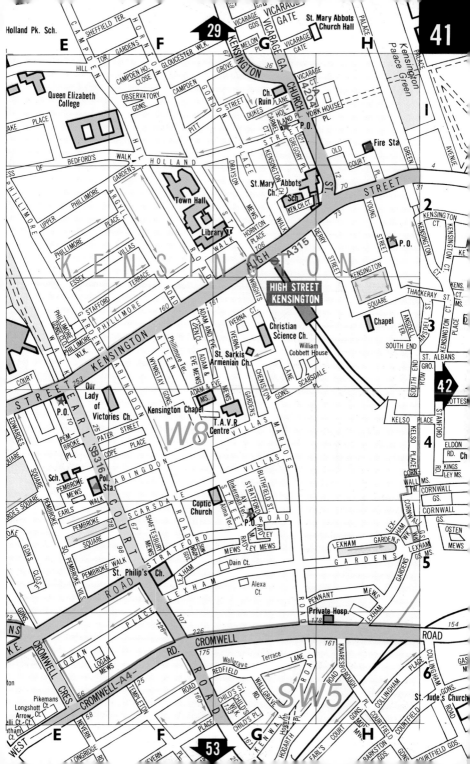

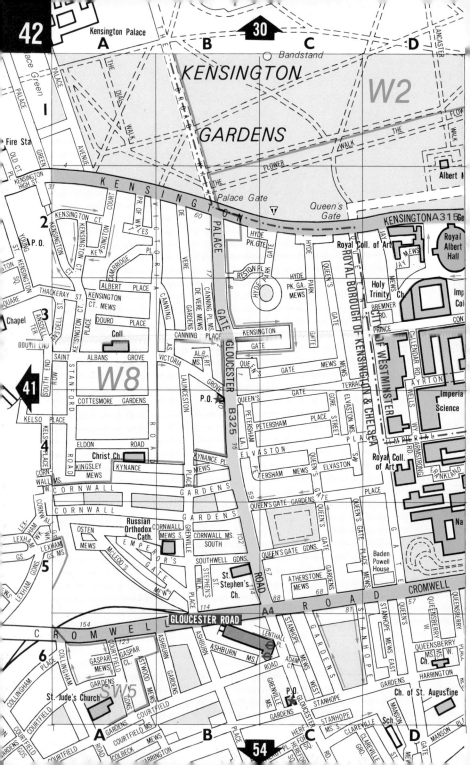

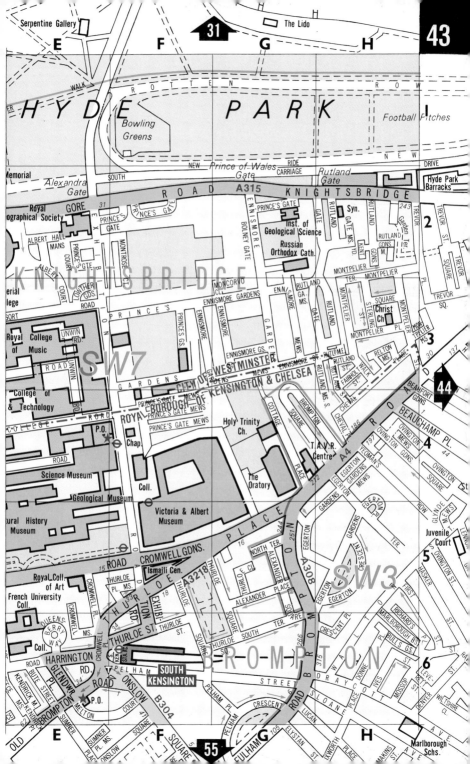

Serpentine Gallery

The Lido

E F **31** G H

H Y D E   P A R K

Bowling
Greens

Football Pitches

Memorial

Alexandra
Gate

Royal
ographical Society

GORE

ALBERT HALL
MANS

ALBERT
COURT

Royal College
of Music

College of
& Technology

Science Museum

Geological Museum

ural History
Museum

Royal Coll.
of Art

French University
Coll.

Coll.

HARRINGTON
RD.

BROMPTON

Prince of Wales
Gate

ROAD

A315

SOUTH

PRINCE'S
GATE

PRINCE'S
GATE

MONTROSE

PRINCE'S
GDNS.

LOWTHER
GDS

PRINCE'S   GATE

ROAD

UNWIN
RD.

UNWIN
RD.

ROAD

ROAD

P.O.

Chap.

COLLEGE

ROAD

PRINCE'S GATE MEWS

PRINCE'S GATE MEWS

PRINCE'S GATE MEWS

BOLNEY GATE

ENNISMORE

ENNISMORE GARDENS

ENNISMORE GS.

Coll.

Victoria & Albert
Museum

CROMWELL GDNS.

Ismaili Cen.

RIDE

Prince of Wales
Gate

CARRIAGE

RRIDE

Rutland
Gate

KNIGHTSBRIDGE

PRINCE'S GATE

Inst. of
Geological Science

Russian
Orthodox Cath.

MONCORVO
CL.

ENNISMORE GARDENS

ENN.
SMORE

GARDENS

WESTMINSTER

CITY OF

BOROUGH OF

ROYAL

KENSINGTON & CHELSEA

Holy Trinity
Ch.

The
Oratory

ENNISMORE ST.

ENNISMORE GS.

MEWS

ENNISMORE ST.

RUTLAND

RUTLAND
MEWS

RUTLAND
GA.
MS.

RUTLAND

GATE

GATE
MS. W.

GATE

RUTLAND
GDNS.

Syn.

KENT

Hyde Park
Barracks

243

243

TREVOR
ST.

Garden Ter.

MONTPELIER

TER.

MONTPELIER

MONTPELIER

STERLING

Christ
Ch

RELTON
MS.

RUTLAND
ST.

RUTLAND

RUTLAND
MS. S.

FAIRHOLT
ST.

CHEVAL PL.

WALK

MONTPELIER

SQUARE

MONTPELIER
PL.

TREVOR
SQUARE

TREVOR
SQ.

2

3

30   137

44

BEAUFORT
GDNS

BEAUCHAMP PL.

OVINGTON
MEWS

OVINGTON GDNS

FOMAN'S

EGERTON
GARDENS

EGERTON
GARDENS

GARDENS

GARDENS

EGERTON

EGERTON
MEWS

OVINGTON
SQUARE

GLYNDE MEWS

ROW

St.

Juvenile
Court

SW3

OVINGTON ST.

HASKER

FIRST

RICHARD'S
BS.

MARLBOROUGH

BULL'S GS.

ST.

ST.

ST.

4

5

6

WESTMINSTER

CHEVAL PL.

COTTAGE

BROMPTON

SQUARE

T.A.V.R.
Centre

A4

272

EGERTON

PLACE

EGERTON
TER.

EGERTON

CRESCENT PL.

CRESCENT

CRESCENT

EGERTON

SW7

THURLOE
PL. MS.

CROMWELL PL.

A3218

THURLOE
PL.

THURLOE

NORTH TER.

F. CL.

ALEXANDER

PLACE

ALEXANDER

SQUARE

THURLOE   SOUTH

THURLOE

THURLOE ST.

THURLOE

EXHIBI-
TION

STA.

QUEEN'S
BERRY
WAY

CROMWELL
MS.

Coll.

GLENDWR
PL.

PELHAM

ROAD

ONSLOW

SQUARE

STREET

SLOANE

DRAYCOTT

BONNIE

ST.

MOSSOP

PENFOLD

ST.

WILTSHIRE
CL.

Marlborough
Schs.

SOUTH
KENSINGTON

P.O.

MELTON

B304

SUMMER
PLACE

ONSLOW

SQUARE

FULHAM

55

BROMPTON

CRESCENT

ELYSTAN

PLACE

LUCAN

SLOANE

AVE.

E F G H

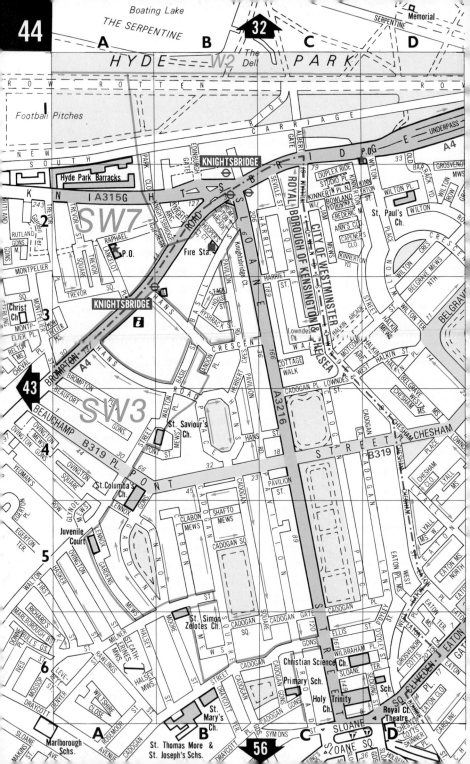

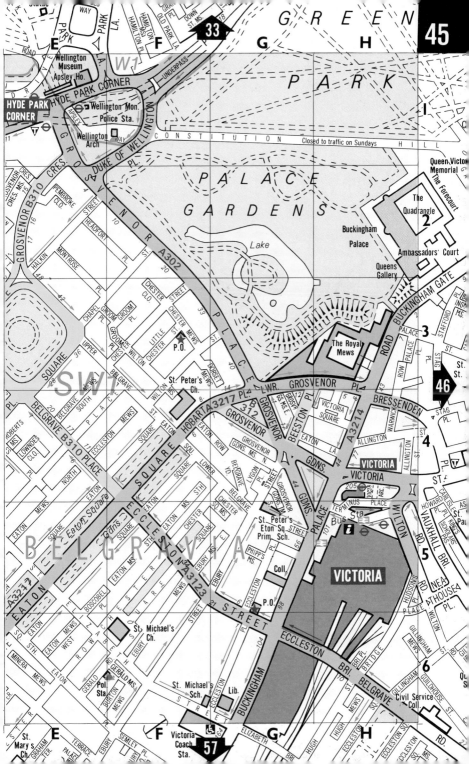

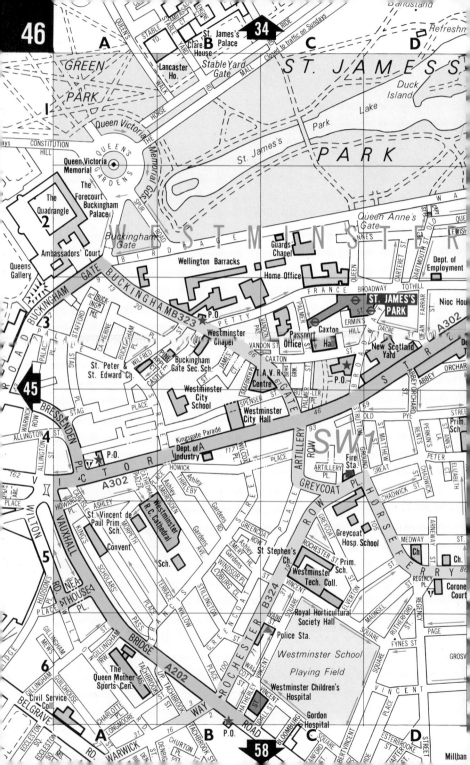

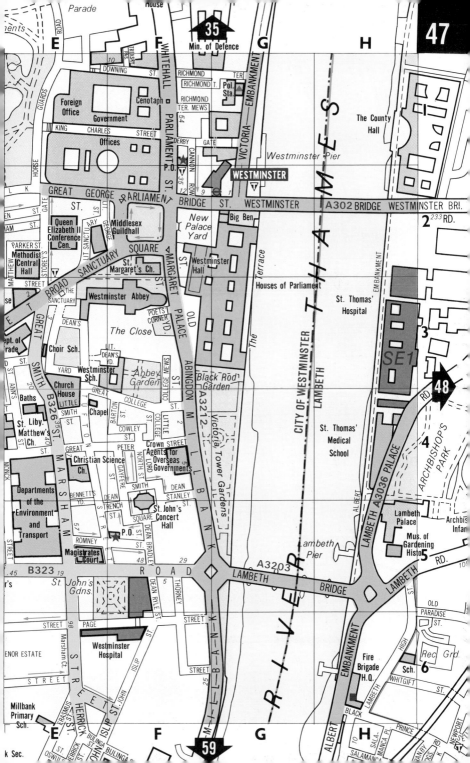

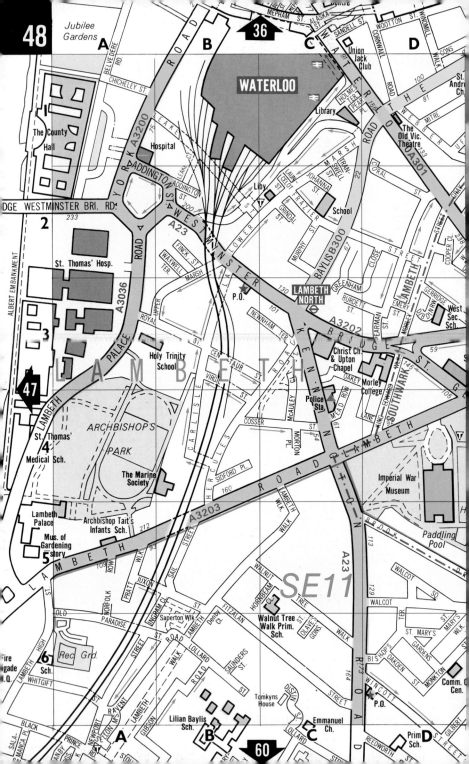

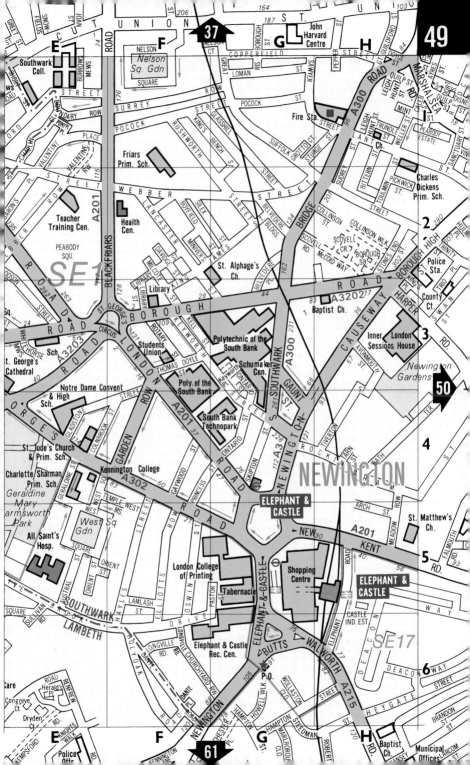

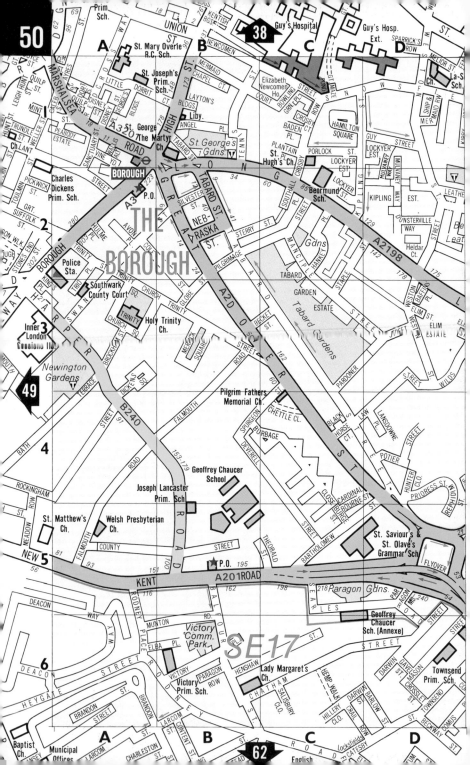

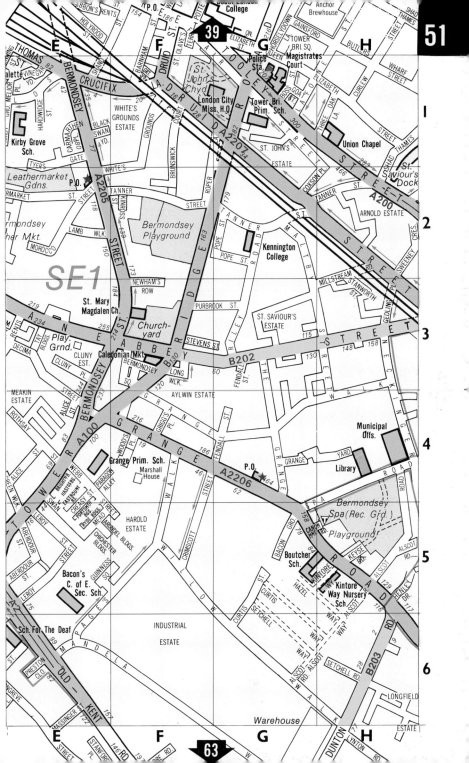

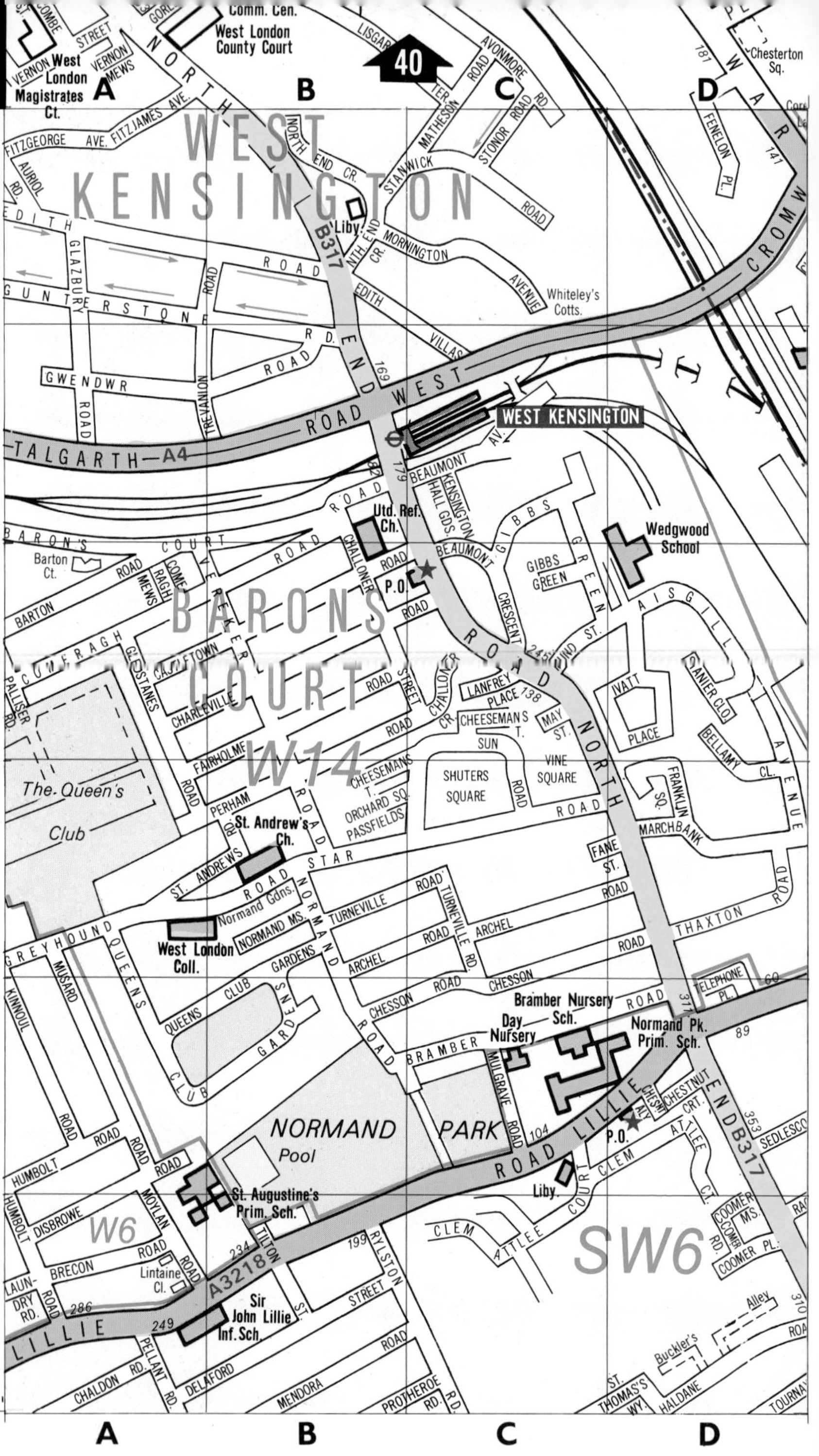

WEST KENSINGTON

KENSINGTON

BARONS COURT W14

NORMAND PARK

W6

SW6

Row A / top:
VERNON STREET
West London Magistrates Ct.
Vernon Mews
West London Mews
Comm. Cen.
West London County Court
AVONMORE ROAD
MATHESON ROAD
STONOR ROAD
Chesterton Sq.
WAR
40

FITZGEORGE AVE.
FITZJAMES AVE.
AUBROL
EDITH
GLAZBURY
GUNTERSTONE
NORTH END CR.
NTH. END CR.
STANWICK RD.
MORNINGTON AVENUE
VILLAS
Whiteley's Cotts.
CROMW
FENELON PL.
181
141

Liby
B317
NORTH END ROAD
EDITH ROAD
GWENDWR ROAD
TREVANION

WEST KENSINGTON

TALGARTH — A4
ROAD WEST
169
179
B317

BARONS COURT
Barton Ct.
Barton Road
COOMB
COMERAGH
PALLISER
GLEDSTANES
CHARLEVILLE
FAIRHOLME
PERHAM
CLAYTON
CASTLETOWN
CHALONER
RD.
BEAUMONT
KENSINGTON HALL GDNS.
BEAUMONT CRESCENT
GIBBS GREEN
GIBBS GREEN ST.
Wedgwood School
Utd. Ref. Ch.
P.O.
AISGILL
STANIER CLO.
BELLAMY
AVENUE

LANFREY PLACE 138
CHEESEMAN'S T.
SUN ROAD
VINE SQUARE
MAY ST.
IVATT PLACE
FRANKLIN SQ.
MARCH BANK
CL.

CHEESEMANS T.
ORCHARD SQ.
PASSFIELDS
SHUTERS SQUARE
STREET
STAR
FANE ST.
THAXTON

The Queen's Club
St. Andrew's Ch.
St. Andrews Road
Normand Gdns.
NORMAND MS.
NORMAND GARDENS
West London Coll.
TURNEVILLE
TURNEVILLE RD.
ARCHEL ROAD
CHESSON ROAD
CHESSON ROAD

GREYHOUND
MUSARD
KINNOUL
QUEENS CLUB GARDENS
CLUB GARDENS
QUEENS CLUB
Bramber Nursery Sch.
Day Nursery
BRAMBER
MILGRAVE ROAD
Normand Pk. Prim. Sch.
TELEPHONE PL.
60
89
353
B317
SEDLESCO
COOMER MS.
COOMER PL.

NORMAND PARK
Pool
St. Augustine's Prim. Sch.
HUMBOLT
DISBROWE
MOYLAN ROAD
TILTON
Lintaine Cl.
BRECON
LAUNDRY RD.
LILLIE
CHALDON RD.
PELLANT RD.
DELAFORD ROAD
MENDORA
Sir John Lillie Inf. Sch.
ROAD LILLIE
104
P.O.
Liby
COURT
ATTLEE
CLEM
CLEM
RYLSTON STREET
PROTHEROE RD.
ST. THOMAS'S WY.
HALDANE
Buckler's
Alley
TOURNA
234
199
286
249
A3218
370
MENDORA ROAD

COURT
ROAD NORTH
ROAD WEST

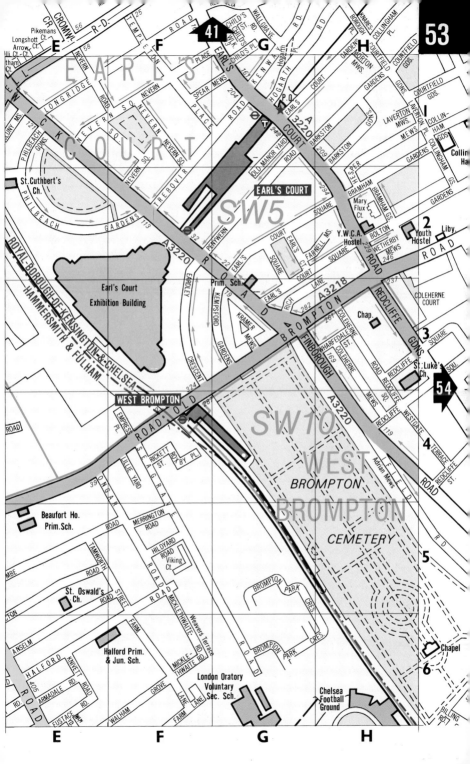

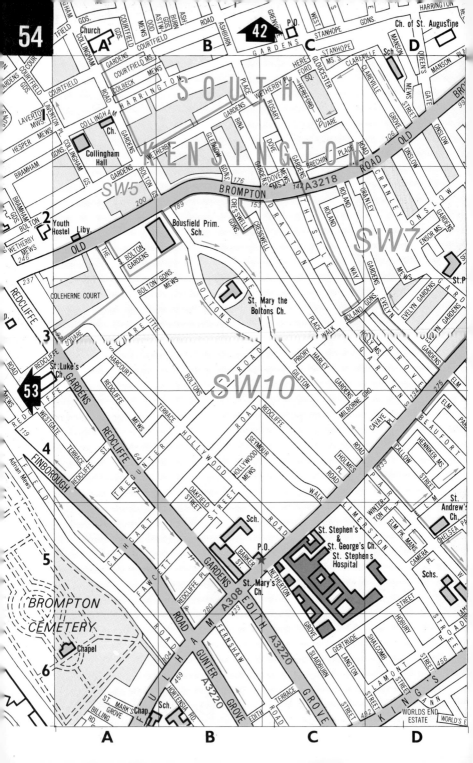

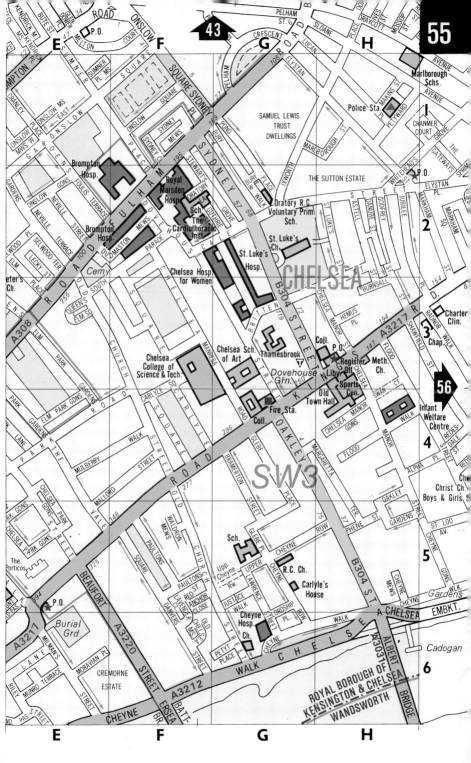

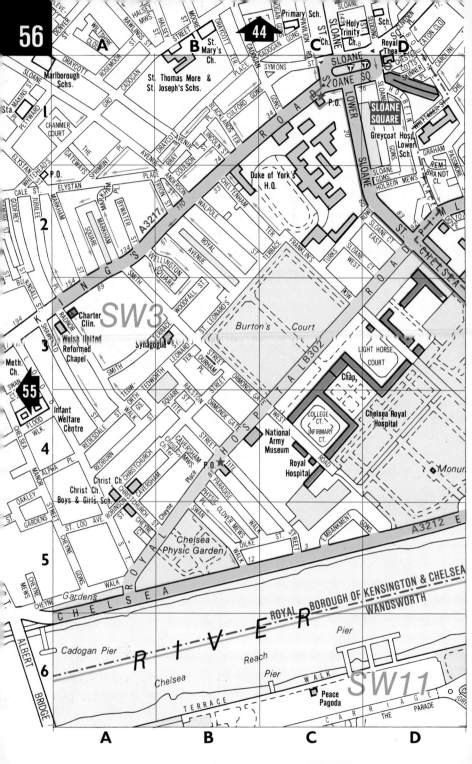

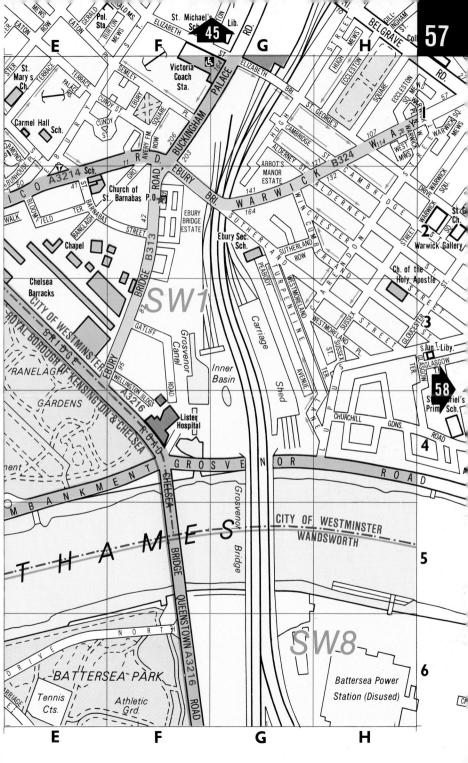

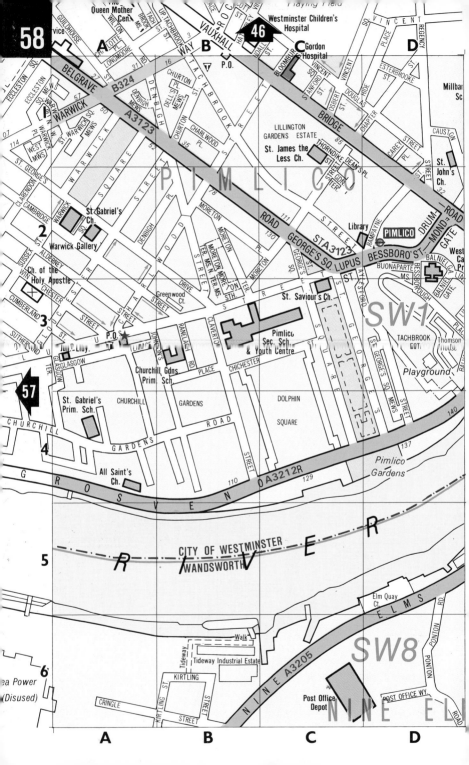

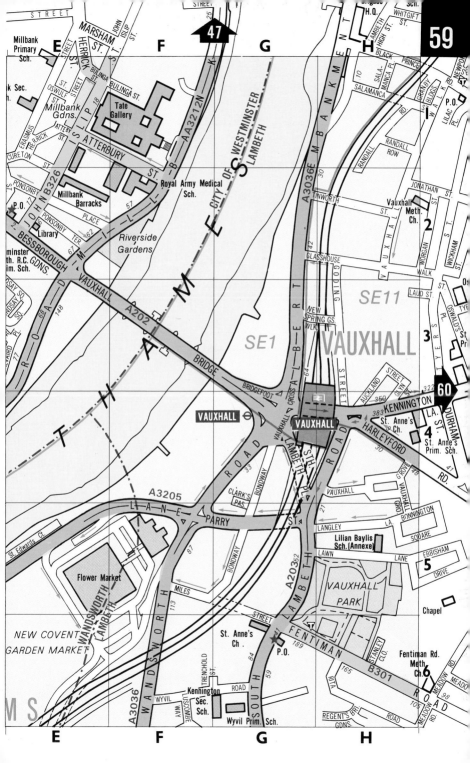

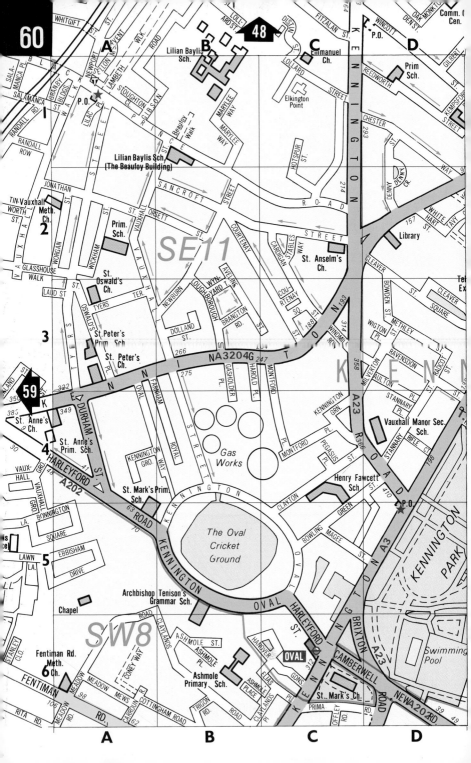

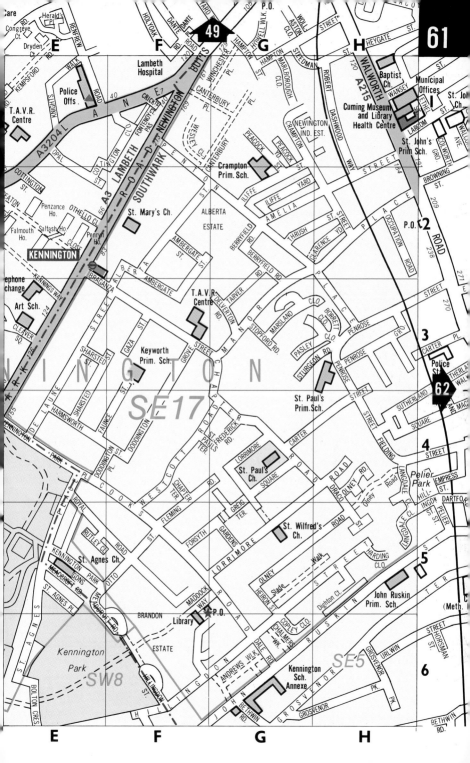

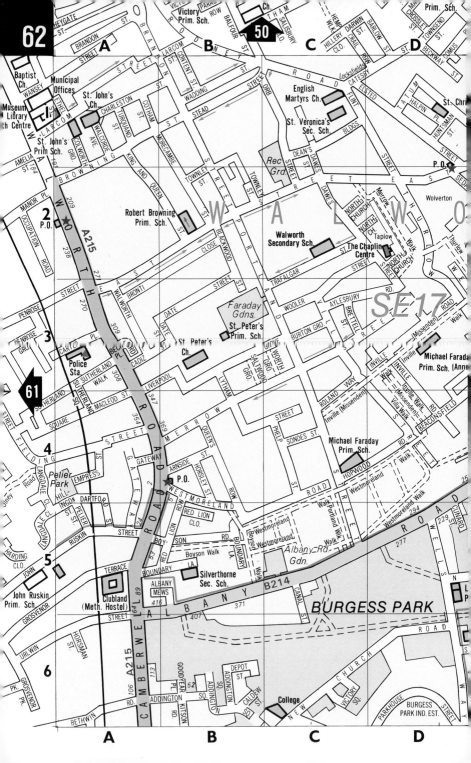

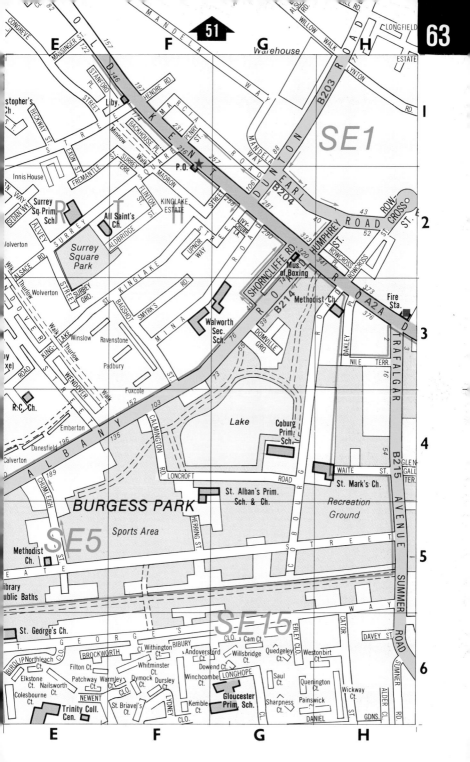

SE1

SE5

SE15

BURGESS PARK

Sports Area

Lake

Surrey
Square
Park

Recreation
Ground

Coburg
Prim.
Sch.

St. Alban's Prim.
Sch. & Ch.

St. Mark's Ch.

WAITE ST.

Walworth
Sec.
Sch.

Methodist Ch.

Mus.
of Boxing

All Saint's
Ch.

Surrey
Sq. Prim.
Sch.

Innis House

P.O.

Lby.

stopher's
Ch.

Fire
Sta.

KINGLAKE
ESTATE

Methodist
Ch.

St. George's Ch.

R.C. Ch.

Library
Public Baths

Gloucester
Prim. Sch.

Trinity Coll.
Cen.

Warehouse

LONGFIELD
ESTATE

WILLOW WALK

MANDELA WAY

CONGREVE

MASSINGER ST.

STANFORD PL.

HENDRE RD.

MARCIA RD.

BACKHOUSE PL.

PENRY ST.

DUNTON ROAD

EARL ROAD

B203 ROAD

LYNTON RD.

ROW-CROSS ST.

ROWCROSS ST.

HUMPHREY ROAD

TRAFALGAR

OAKLEY

NILE TERR.

GLEN-GALL
TER.

B215 AVENUE

SUMMER ROAD

SUMNER ROAD

CATOR

DAVEY ST.

MANDELA WAY

A2A

B204

B214

SHORNCLIFFE RD.

DOMVILLE GRO.

COBOURG ROAD

STREET

HERRING ST.

CALMINGTON RD.

LONCROFT

ALBANY

WENDOVER

GREEN

SURREY

SURREY GRO.

KINGLAKE

SMYRK'S RD.

MINA ST.

BASSHOT

UPNOR WAY

IVY
CHUR
LA.

ST. JAMES ST.

STREET

MADRON

FLINTON ST.

SURREY TERR.

MINNOW WALK

EXON ST.

FREMANTLE

BECKWAY ST.

ALVEY ST.

WALSAGE RD.

THURLOW

WINSLOW

THURLOW

KING'S

Wolverton

Wolverton

Ravenstone

Padbury

Foxcote

Emberton

Danesfield

Calverton

Aldbridge

SEDAN WY.

HANDOVER

WALK

Winchcombe
Ct.

LONGHOPE

Kemble
Ct.

Dursley
Ct.

Dymock
Ct.

LYDNEY

St. Briavel's
Ct.

NEWENT

Colesbourne
Ct.

Elkstone
Ct.

Patchway
Ct.

Warmley
Ct.

Nailsworth
Ct.

Filton Ct.

Northleach
Ct.

BIRDLIP

Brockworth
Ct.

Whitminster
Ct.

Withington
Ct.

BIBURY

Andoversford
Ct.

Dowend Ct.

Willsbridge
Ct.

Quedgeley
Ct.

Weston birt
Ct.

Saul
Ct.

Sharpness
Ct.

Painswick
Ct.

Quenington
Ct.

Wickway
Ct.

DANIEL

ALDER CT.

GDNS.

GEORGE'S

GATE

E   F   G   H

E   F   G   H   I

INDEX TO STREETS

HOW TO USE THIS ATLAS

1. Each street name is followed by its Postal District and then by its map reference; e.g. Abbey Gdns. NW8—3C 6 is in the North West 8 Postal District and is to be found in map square 3C on page 6.

2. A strict alphabetical order is followed in which Av., Rd., St. etc. (though abbreviated) are read in full and as part of the street name; e.g. Abbey Orchard St. appears after Abbey Gdns. M., but before Abbey Rd.

3. With the now general usage of Postal Coding, it is not recommended that this index be used as a means of addressing mail.

ABBREVIATIONS USED IN THIS ATLAS

All: Alley
App: Approach
Arc: Arcade
Av: Avenue
Boulevd: Boulevard
Bri: Bridge
B'way: Broadway
Bldgs: Buildings
Chu: Church
Chyd: Churchyard
Cir: Circus
Circ: Circle
Clo: Close
Comn: Common
Cotts: Cottages
Ct: Court
Cres: Crescent
Dri: Drive

E: East
Embkmt: Embankment
Est: Estate
Gdns: Gardens
Ga: Gate
Gt: Great
Grn: Green
Gro: Grove
Ho: House
Junct: Junction
La: Lane
Lit: Little
Lwr: Lower
Mnr: Manor
Mans: Mansions
Mkt: Market
M: Mews
Mt: Mount

N: North
Pal: Palace
Pde: Parade
Pk: Park
Pas: Passage
Pl: Place
Rd: Road
S: South
Sq: Square
Sta: Station
St: Street
Ter: Terrace
Up: Upper
Vs: Villas
Wlk: Walk
W: West
Yd: Yard

Abbey Gdns. NW8—3C 6
Abbey Orchard St. SW1—4D 46
Abbey Rd. NW8—1B 6
Abbey St. SE1—3F 51
Abbotsbury Clo. W14—2B 40
Abbotsbury Rd. W14—1B 40
Abbots La. SE1—6F 39
Abbot's Mnr. Est. SW1—2G 57
Abchurch La. EC4—2C to 1C 38
Abchurch Yd. EC4—2C 38
Abercorn Clo. NW8—4C 6
Abercorn Pl. NW8—4B 6
Aberdeen Pl. NW8—2D 18
Aberdour St. SE1—5E 51
Abingdon Rd. W8—3F 41
Abingdon St. SW1—3F 47
Abingdon Vs. W8—4F 41
Abinger M. W9—1E 17
Acacia Gdns. NW8—2E 7
Acacia Pl. NW8—2F 7
Acacia Rd. NW8—2E 7
Academy Bldgs. N1—4E 15
Achilles Way. W1—6E 33
Acklam Rd. W10—5B 16
Acton St. WC1—5H 11
Adair Rd. W10—2B 16
Adam Ct. SW7—6C 42
Adam & Eve Ct. W1—6B 22
Adam & Eve M. W8—3F 41
Adam's Ct. EC2—6D 26
Adam's Row. W1—3E 33
Adam St. WC2—3G 35
Addington Sq. SE5—6B 62
Addington St. SE1—2A 48
Addison Bri. Pl. W14—5B 40
Addison Cres. W14—3A 40
Addison Rd. W14—1A to 4C 40
Addle Hill. EC4—1G 37
Addle St. EC2—5A 26
Adelaide St. WC2—3F 35
Adeline Pl. WC1—5D 22
Adelphi Ter. WC2—4G 35
Adpar St. W2—3G 19
Adrian M. SW10—4H 53
Affleck St. N1—3A 12
Agar St. WC2—3G 35
Agdon St. EC1—1F 25
Airlie Gdns. W8—6E 29
Air St. W1—3B 34
Aisgill Av. W14—3D 52

Alaska St. SE1—6C 36
Albany. W1—3B 34
Albany Ct. Yd. W1—4B 34
Albany M. SE5—5B 62
Albany Rd. SE5—5B 62 to 2G 63
Albany St. NW1—2G 9
Albany Ter. NW1—2G 21
  (in two parts)
Alba Pl. W11—6B 16
Albemarle St. W1—3H 33
Albemarle Way. EC1—2F 25
Alberta Est. SE17—2F 61
Alberta St. SE17—2F 61
Albert Bri. SW3 & SW11—6H 55
Albert Ct. SW7—2E 43
Albert Embkmt. SE1—3G 59 to 2H 47
Albert Ga. SW1—1C 44
Albert Hall Mans. SW7—2E 43
Albert M. SW8—3B 42
Albert Pl. W8—3A 42
Albert Rd. NW6—3C 4
Albert St. NW1—1G 9
Albert Ter. NW1—1D 8
Albion Clo. W2—2H 31
Albion M. W2—1H 31
Albion Pl. EC1—3F 25
Albion Pl. EC2—5C 26
Albion St. W2—1H 31
Aldbridge St. SE17—2F 63
Aldenham St. NW1—4C 10
Alder Clo. SE15—6H 63
Aldermanbury. EC2—5A 26
Aldermanbury Sq. EC2—5A 26
Aldermans Wlk. EC2—5E 27
Alderney St. SW1—1G 57 to 3A 58
Aldersgate St. EC1—3H 25
Alderson St. W10—1A 16
Aldford St. W1—4D 32
Aldgate. EC3—1G 39
Aldgate Av. E1—6G 27
Aldgate High St. EC3—1G 39
Aldridge Rd. Vs. W11—4D 16
Aldsworth Clo. W9—3G 17
Aldwych. WC2—1A 36
Alexa Ct. W8—5G 41
Alexander M. W2—6G 17
Alexander Pl. SW7—5G 43
Alexander Sq. SW3—5G 43
Alexander St. W2—5G 17
Alford Pl. N1—4A 14

Alfred M. W1—6C 22
Alfred Pl. WC1—4C 22
Alfred Rd. W2—4F 17
Algernon Rd. NW6—1E 5
Alice St. SE1—4E 51
Alie St. E1—1H 39
Allen St. W8—3F 41
Allhallows La. EC4—3B 38
Allingham St. N1—2G 13
Allington Rd. W10—4A 4
Allington St. SW1—4H 45
Allitsen Rd. NW8—3F 7
All Saints Rd. W11—5C 16
All Saints St. N1—2H 11
Allsop Pl. NW1—2C 20
All Souls' Pl. W1—5H 21
Alma Sq. NW8—4C 6
Alma Ter. W8—5G 41
Alperton St. W10—1B 16
Alpha Clo. NW1—6H 7
Alpha Pl. NW6—2F 5
Alpha Pl. SW3—4H 55
Alsace Rd. SE17—2E 63
Alscot Rd. SE1—6G 51
  (in two parts)
Alscot Way. SE1—6G 51
Alvey St. SE17—2E 63
Ambassadors' Ct. SW1—6B 34
Ambergate St. SE17—2F 61
Amberley Rd. W9—3G 17
Ambrosden Av. SW1—4B 46
Amelia St. SE17—2G 61
Amen Corner. EC4—6G 25
Amen Ct. EC4—6F 25
America Sq. EC3—2G 39
America St. SE1—6H 37
Ampthill Est. NW1—3B 10
Ampton Pl. WC1—5A 12
Ampton St. WC1—6A 12
Amwell St. EC1—4C 12
Anchor Brewhouse. SE1—6H 39
Anchor Yd. EC1—1A 26
Anderson St. SW3—2B 56
Andover Pl. NW6—2H 5
Andoversford Ct. SE15—6F 63
Andrew Borde St. WC2—6E 23
Andrewes Ho. EC2—4B 26
Andrews Crosse. WC2—1C 36
Andrews Wlk. SE17—6G 61
Angel Ct. EC2—6C 26

Angel Ct. SW1—5B 34
Angel M. N1—3D 12
Angel Pas. EC4—3C 38
Angel Pl. SE1—1B 50
Angel Sq. N1—3E 13
Angel St. EC1—6H 25
Anning St. EC2—1F 27
Ann La. SW10—6D 54
Ann's Clo. SW1—2C 44
Ann's Pl. E1—5H 27
Ansdell St. W8—3A 42
Ansdell Ter. W8—3H 41
Anselm Rd. SW6—6E 53
Apothecary St. EC4—1F 37
Appleby St. E2—2H 15
Appleford Rd. W10—2A 16
Apple Tree Yd. SW1—4C 34
Appold St. EC2—3E 27
Apsley Way. W1—1E 45
Aquila St. NW8—2F 7
Aquinas St. SE1—5D 36
Arcade, The. EC2—5E 27
Archel Rd. W14—4B & 4C 52
Archer St. W1—2C 34
Archery Clo. W2—1A 32
Arches, The. WC2—4G 35
Archibald M. W1—4F 33
Arch St. SE1—5H 49
Arden Est. N1—3E 13
Argyle Sq. WC1—5G 11
Argyle St. WC1—5F to 5H 11
Argyle Wlk. WC1—5G 11
Argyll Rd. W8—2F 41
Argyll St. W1—6A 22
Arlington Av. N1—1A 14
Arlington Rd. NW1—1H 9
Arlington Sq. N1—1A 14
Arlington St. SW1—5A 34
Arlington Way. EC1—5D 12
Armadale Rd. SW6—6E 53
Armstrong Rd. SW7—4D 42
Arne St. WC2—1G 35
Arneway St. SW1—5D 46
Arnold Cir. E2—6G 15
Arnold Est. SE1—2H 51
Arnside St. SE17—4B 62
Arrow Ct. SW5—1E 53
Artesian Rd. W2—1E 29
Arthur St. EC4—3C 38
Artillery La. E1—4F 27
Artillery Pas. E1—4G 27
Artillery Pl. SW1—4C 46
Artillery Row. SW1—4C 46
Artizan St. E1—5G 27
Arundel Bldgs. SE1—5F 51
Arundel Gdns. W11—2B 28
Arundel St. WC2—2B 36
Ashbridge St. NW8—2G 19
Ashburn Gdns. SW7—6B 42
Ashburn M. SW7—6B 42
Ashburn Pl. SW7—6B 42
Ashby St. EC1—5F 13
Ashentree Ct. EC4—1D 36
Ashford Pl. N1—5E 15
Ashford St. N1—4E 15
Ashland Pl. W1—4D 20
Ashley Gdns. SW1—5B 46
(in three parts)
Ashley Pl. SW1—5A 46
Ashmill St. NW1—3G 19
Ashmole Pl. SW8—6B 60
Ashmole St. SW8—6B 60
Ashmore Rd. W9—4C 4
Ashworth Rd. W9—5H 5
Aske St. N1—4E 15
Astell St. SW3—2H 59
Astwood M. SW7—6A 42
Athens Gdns. W9—2D 16
Atherstone M. SW7—5C 42
Atterbury St. SW1—1E 59
Attneave St. WC1—6C 12
Aubrey Pl. NW8—3B 6
Aubrey Rd. W8—5C 28
Aubrey Wlk. W8—6D 28
Auckland St. SE11—4H 59
Audley Sq. W1—5F 33
Augustus St. NW1—4H 9
Aulton Pl. SE11—3D 60

Auriol Rd. W14—1A 52
Austin Friars. EC2—6D 26
Austin Friars Pas. EC2—6D 26
Austin Friars Sq. EC2—6D 26
Austin St. E2—5G 15
Austral St. SE11—5E 49
Aveline St. SE11—2B 60
Ave Maria La. EC4—1G 37
Avenue Clo. NW8—1H 7
Avenue Rd. NW8—1G 7
Avery Farm Row. SW1—1F 57
Avery Row. W1—2G 33
Avonmore Pl. W14—5B 40
Avonmore Rd. W14—6B 40
Avonmouth St. SE1—3H 49
Avon Pl. SE1—2A 50
Axe Ct. E2—4G 15
Aybrook St. W1—4E 21
Aylesbury Rd. SE17—3C 62
Aylesbury St. EC1—2E 25
Aylesford St. SW1—3D 58
Aylwin Est. SE1—4F 51
Ayres St. SE1—1A 50
Ayrton Rd. SW7—3D 42

Babmaes St. SW1—4C 34
Bacchus Wlk. N1—3E 15
Bache's St. N1—5D 14
Back All. EC3—1G 39
Back Hill. EC1—2D 24
Backhouse Pl. SE17—1F 63
Bacon Gro. SE1—5G 51
Bacon St. E1—1H 27
Baden Pl. SE1—1C 50
Baffins Pl. SE1—3D 50
Bagshot St. SE17—3F 63
Bainbridge St. WC1—5E 23
Baird St. EC1—1A 26
Bakers Hall Ct. EC3—3E 39
Baker's M. W1—6D 20
Baker's Rents. E2—5G 15
Baker's Row. EC1—2C 24
Baker St.—2C 20
W1 1-133 & 2-136
NW1 remainder
Balcombe St. NW1—1A to 3B 20
Balderton St. W1—1E 33
Baldwin's Gdns. EC1—4C 24
Baldwin St. EC1—6B 14
Baldwin Ter. N1—2H 13
Balfe St. N1—3H 11
Balfour M. W1—4E 33
Balfour Pl. W1—4E 33
Balfour St. SE17—5B 50
Ball Ct. EC3—1D 38
Balniel Ga. SW1—2D 58
Baltic St. EC1—2H 25
Balvaird Pl. SW1 SW1—3D 58
Banbury Ct. WC2—2F 35
Bank End. SE1—4B 38
Bankside. SE1—4H 37
Banner St. EC1—2A 26
Barbara Brosnan Ct. NW8—3D 6
Barbican. EC2—4A 26
Barbon Clo. WC1—3H 23
Barfett St. W10—1B 16
Barford St. N1—1D 12
Barge Ho. St. SE1—4D 36
Baring St. N1—1B 14
Barker St. SW10—5B 54
Bark Pl. W2—2H 29
Barkston Gdns. SW5—1H 53
Barleymow Pas. EC1—4G 25
Barlow Pl. W1—3H 33
Barlow St. SE17—6D 50
Barnard's Inn. EC1—5D 24
Barnby St. NW1—4B 10
Barnham St. SE1—1F 51
Barnsbury Rd. N1—2C 12
Barnsdale Rd. W9—1D 16
Barnwood Clo. W9—3H 17
Baron Clo. N1—2C 12
Baroness Rd. E2—4H 15
Baron's Ct. Rd. W14—2A 52
Baron's Pl. SE1—2E 49

Baron St. N1—2C 12
Barrett St. W1—1E 33
Barrie Est. W2—2D 30
Barrow Hill Est. NW8—3G 7
Barrow Hill Rd. NW8—3G 7
Barter St. WC1—5G 23
Bartholomew Clo. EC1—4G 25
Bartholomew Ct. EC1—1A 26
Bartholomew La. EC2—6C 26
Bartholomew Pl. EC1—4H 25
Bartholomew Sq. EC1—6A 14
Bartholomew St. SE1—5C 50
Bartlett Ct. EC4—5D 24
Barton Ct. W14—3A 52
Barton Rd. W14—3A 52
Barton St. SW1—4F 47
Basil St. SW3—3B 44
(in two parts)
Basinghall Av. EC2—5B 26
Basinghall St. EC2—5B 26
Basing Ho. Yd. E2—5F 15
Basing Pl. E2—4F 15
Basing St. W11—5B 16
Bassishaw Highwalk. EC2—5B 26
Bastwick St. EC1—1G 25
Batchelor St. N1—1D 12
Bateman's Bldgs. W1—1D 34
Bateman's Row. EC2—6F 15
Bateman St. W1—1D 34
Bath Ct. EC1—2C 24
Bath Ct. Clo. EC1—6E 15
Bath Pl. EC1—6E 15
Bath St. EC1—5B 14
Bath Ter. SE1—4H 49
Bathurst M. W2—2E 31
Bathurst St. W2—2E 31
Battersea Bri. SW3—6F 55
Battle Bri. La. SE1—5E 39
Battle Bri. Rd. NW1—3F 11
Bayham Pl. NW1—2B 10
Bayham St. NW1—1A 10
Bayley St. WC1—4D 22
Baylis Rd. SE1—2C 48
Bayswater Rd. W2—4H 29 to 2B 32
Beaconsfield Rd. SE17—4D 62
Beak St. W1—2B 34
Bear All. EC4—6E 25
Bear Gdns. SE1—4H 37
Bear La. SE1—5F 37
Bear St. WC2—3E 35
Beatty St. NW1—2A 10
Beauchamp Pl. SW3—4H 43
Beauchamp St. EC1—4C 24
Beaufort Gdns. SW3—4A 44
Beaufort St. SW3—4D 54 to 6F 55
Beaufoy Wlk. SE11—1B 60
Beaumont Av. W14—2C 52
Beaumont Cres. W14—3C 52
Beaumont M. W1—4E 21
Beaumont Pl. W1—1B 22
Beaumont St. W1—3E 21
Becket St. SE1—3C 50
Beckford Pl. SE17—3A 62
Beckway St. SE1—1D 62 & 1E 63
Bedale St. SE1—5B 38
Bedford Av. WC1—5D 22
Bedfordbury. WC2—3F 35
Bedford Ct. WC2—3F 35
Bedford Gdns. W8—6E 29
Bedford Pas. W1—3B 22
Bedford Pl. WC1—3F 23
Bedford Row. WC1—3A 24
Bedford Sq. WC1—4D 22
Bedford St. WC2—2F 35
Bedford Way. WC1—2E 23
Beech St. EC2—3H 25
Beeston Pl. SW1—4G 45
Beethoven St. W10—4A 4
Belgrave Gdns. NW8—1A 6
Belgrave M. N. SW1—3D 44
Belgrave M. S. SW1—4E 45
Belgrave M. W. SW1—3D 44
Belgrave Pl. SW1—4E 45
Belgrave Rd. SW1—6H 45
Belgrave Sq. SW1—3D 44
Belgrave Yd. SW1—4G 45
Belgrove St. WC1—4G 11
Bellamy Clo. W14—3D 52

Bell Inn Yd. EC3—1D 38
Bell La. E1—4G 27
Bell St. NW1—4G 19
Bell Wharf La. EC4—3B 38
Belsize Rd. NW6—1G 5
Belvedere Bldgs. SE1—2G 49
Belvedere Pl. SE1—3G 49
Belvedere Rd. SE1—6A 36
Bendall M. NW1—3H 19
Bengal Ct. EC3—1D 38
Benjamin St. EC1—3E 25
Ben Johnson Ho. EC2—3A 26
Bennet's Hill. EC4—2G 37
Bennet St. SW1—5A 34
Bennett's Yd. SW1—4E 47
Bentinck M. W1—5F 21
Bentinck St. W1—5F 21
Berkeley Gdns. W8—5G 29
Berkeley M. W1—6C 20
Berkeley Sq. W1—3G 33
Berkeley St. W1—4H 33
Bermondsey Sq. SE1—3F 51
Bermondsey St. SE1—6E 39 to 4E 51
Bernard St. WC1—2F 23
Berners M. W1—5B 22
Berners Pl. W1—5C 22
Berners Rd. N1—1E 13
Berners St. W1—5B 22
Berryfield Rd. SE17—2G 61
Berry Pl. EC1—6F 13
Berry St. EC1—1G 25
Berwick St. W1—6B 22
Bessborough Gdns. SW1—2E 59
Bessborough Pl. SW1—3D 58
Bessborough St. SW1—2D 58
Bethnal Grn. Rd. E1—1G 27
Bethwin Rd. SE5—6G 61 & 6A 62
Betterton St. WC2—6G 23
Bevan St. N1—1A 14
Bevenden St. N1—4C 14
Bevington Rd. W10—4A 16
Bevin Way. WC1—4B 12
Bevis Marks. EC3—6F 27
Bibury Clo. SE15—6F 63
Bickenhall St. W1—3B 20
Bidborough St. WC1—5E 11
Biddulph Mans. W9—6H 5
Biddulph Rd. W9—5H 5
Billing Rd. SW10—6A 54
Billiter Sq. EC3—1F 39
Billiter St. EC3—1F 39
Bina Gdns. SW5—1B 54
Bingham Pl. W1—3D 20
Binney St. W1—1E 33
Birchin La. EC3—1D 38
Birdcage Wlk. SW1—2A 46
Birdlip Clo. SE15—6E 63
Bird St. W1—1E 33
Birkenhead St. WC1—4G 11
Bishop King's Rd. W14—5A 40
Bishop's Bri. Rd. W2—6A 18
Bishop's Ct. EC4—6F 25
Bishop's Ct. WC2—6C 24
Bishopsgate. EC2—6E 27
Bishopsgate Chu. Yd. EC2—5E 27
Bishop's Ter. SE11—6D 48
Bittern St. SE1—2H 49
Blackall St. EC2—1D 26
Blackburne's M. W1—2D 32
Blackfriars Bri. SE1 & EC4—3E 37
Black Friars Ct. EC4—2F 37
Black Friars La. EC4—2F 37
Blackfriars Pas. EC4—2F 37
Blackfriars Rd. SE1—2F 49
Blackfriars Underpass. EC4—1E 37
Black Horse Ct. SE1—4C 50
Blacklands Ter. SW3—1B 56
Black Prince Rd. SE1 & SE11—6H 47
Black Swan Yd. SE1—1E 51
Blackwood St. SE17—2B 62
Blagrove Rd. W10—4B 16
Blandford Sq. NW1—2A 20
Blandford St. W1—5C 20
Bleeding Heart Yd. EC1—4D 24
Blemheim M. W1—2C 6
Blenheim Cres. W11—2A 28
Blenheim Pas. NW8—2B 6
Blenheim St. W1—1G 33

Blenheim Ter. NW8—2B 6
Bletchley St. N1—3B 14
Bletsoe Wlk. N1—2A 14
Blithfield St. W8—4G 41
Blomfield Rd. W9—3A 18
Blomfield St. EC2—5D 26
Blomfield Vs. W2—4A 18
Bloomburg ST. SW1—1C 58
Bloomfield Pl. W1—2H 33
Bloomfield Ter. SW1—2E 57
Bloomsbury Pl. WC1—5G 23
Bloomsbury Pl. WC1—4G 23
Bloomsbury Sq. WC1—4G 23
Bloomsbury St. WC1—4E 23
Bloomsbury Way. WC1—5G 23
Blore Ct. W1 W1—1C 34
Blossom St. E1—3G 27
Blue Ball Yd. W1—5A 34
Boadicea St. N1—1H 11
Bolney Ga. SW7—2G 43
Bolsover St. W1—2H 21
Bolt Ct. EC4—6D 24
Bolton Cres. SE5—6E 61
Bolton Gdns. SW5—2H 53
Bolton Gdns. M. SW10—3A 54
Bolton Rd. NW8—1A 6
Boltons, The. SW10—3B 54
Bolton St. W1—5H 33
Bond St. (New) W1—1G 33
Bond St. (Old) W1—4A 34
Bondway. SW8—5G & 4G 59
Bonhill St. EC2—2D 26
Bonnington Sq. SW8—5H 59
Book M. WC2—6E 23
Booth's Pl. W1—5B 22
Boot St. N1—6E 15
Boreas Wlk. N1—3G 13
Borough High St. SE1—2A 50
Borough Rd. SE1—3F 49
Borough Sq. SE1—2H 49
Borrett Clo. SE17—3H 61
Boscobel Pl. SW1—5B 45
Boscobel St. NW8—3E 19
Boss St. SE1—1G 51
Boston Pl. NW1—2A 20
Boswell Ct. WC1—3H 23
Boswell St. WC1—3G 23
Bosworth Rd. W10—5H 5
Botolph All. EC3—3D 38
Botolph La. EC3—3D 38
Botts M. W2—1F 29
Bourchier St. W1-2D 34
Boundary La. SE17—5A & 5B 62
Boundary Pas. E2—1G 27
Boundary Rd. NW8—1A 6
Boundary Row. SE1—1E 49
Boundary St. E2—6G 15
Bourdon Pl. W1—3G 33
Bourdon St. W1—3G 33
Bourlet Clo. W1—4A 22
Bourne Est. EC1—3C 24
Bourne St. SW1—6D 44
Bourne Ter. W2—4H 17
Bouverie Pl. W2—5F 19
Bouverie St. EC4—1D 36
Bow Chyd. EC4—1A 38
Bowden St. SE11—3D 60
Bowland Yd. SW1—2C 44
Bow La. EC4—1A 38
Bowl Ct. EC2—2F 27
Bowling Grn. La. EC1—1D 24
Bowling Grn. Pl. SE1—1C 50
Bowling Grn. St. SE11—5C 60
Bowling Grn. Wlk. N1—5E 15
Bow St. WC2—1G 35
Boyce St. SE1—6B 36
Boyfield St. SE1—2F 49
Boyle St. W1—2A 34
Boyne Ter. M. W11—5C 28
Boyson Rd. SE17—5B 62
Boyson Wlk. SE17—5B 62
Brabant Ct. EC3—2D 38
Brackley St. EC1—3A 26
Bracklyn St. N1—2B 14
Braden St. W9—2H 17
Bradiston Rd. W9—5D 4
Bradley's Clo. N1—3D 12
Brad St. SE1—6D 36

Braganza St. SE17—3E 61
Braham St. E1—6H 27
Braidwood St. SE1—6E 39
Bramber Rd. W14—5C 52
Bramerton St. SW3—4G 55
Bramham Gdns. SW5—2H 53
Brandon Est. SE17—6F 61
Brandon M. EC2—4B 26
Brandon St. SE17—6A 50
Brangton Rd. SE11—3B 60
Bravington Pl. W9—1B 16
Bravington Rd. W9—4B 4
Bray Pl. SW3—1B 56
Bread St. EC4—2A 38
Bream's Bldgs. EC4—6C 24
Brechin Pl. SW7—1C 54
Brecon Rd. W6—6A 52
Bremner Rd. SW7—3D 42
Brendon St. W1—5H 19
Bressenden Pl. SW1—4H 45
Breton Ho. EC1—3A 26
Brettell St. SE17—3C 62
Brewer's Grn. SW1—3C 46
Brewer St. W1—3B 34
Brewhouse Yd. EC1—1F 25
Briar Wlk. W10—6A 4
Brick Ct. EC4—1C 36
Brick La. E2—6H 15
Brick St. W1—6F 33
Bride Ct. EC4—1E 37
Bride La. EC4—1E 37
Bridewell Pl. EC4—1E 37
Bridford M. W1—3G 21
Bridgefoot. SE1—3G 59
Bridgeman St. NW8—3G 7
Bridge Pl. SW1—6H 45
Bridgeway St. NW1—2C 10
Bridge St. SW1—2F 47
Bridgewater Highwalk. EC2—3H 25
Bridgewater Sq. EC2—3H 25
Bridgewater St. EC2—3H 25
Bridgeway St. NW1—2C 10
Bridge Yd. SE1—5D 38
Bridle La. W1—2B 34
Bridport Pl. N1—1C & 2C 14
Bridstow Pl. W2—6F 17
Brighton Bldgs. SE1—4E 51
Brill Pl. NW1—3E 11
Brinton Wlk. SE1—6F 37
Briset St. EC1—3F 25
Bristol Gdns. W9—3A 18
Bristol M. W9—2A 18
Britannia St. WC1—5H 11
Britannia Wlk. N1—5B 14
Britten St. SW3—3G 55
Britton St. EC1—2E 25
Brixton Rd. SW9—6C 60
Broadbent St. W1—2G 33
Broad Ct. WC2—1G 35
Broadgate. EC2—4E 27
Broadgate Circ. EC2—4E 27
Broadley St. NW8—3F 19
Broadley Ter. NW1—2H 19
Broad Sanctuary. SW1—3E 47
Broadstone Pl. W1—4D 20
Broad St. Av. EC2—5D 26
Broad St. Pl. EC2—5D 26
Broad Wlk. NW1—1E 9 to 1F 21
Broad Wlk. W2 & W1—3C 32
Broad Wlk., The. W8—6A 30
Broadwall. SE1—4D 36
Broadway. SW1—3C 46
Broadwick St. W1—1B 34
Broadwood Ter. W14—6D 40
Broad Yd. EC1—3E 25
Brockham St. SE1—3A 50
Brockworth Clo. SE15—6E 63
Broken Wharf. EC4—2H 37
Bromfield St. N1—2D 12
Bromley Pl. W1—3A 22
Brompton Arc. SW3—2B 44
Brompton Pk. Cres. SW6—5G 53
Brompton Pl. SW3—3A 44
Brompton Rd. SW3 & SW1—6G 43
Brompton Sq. SW3—4G 43
Brondesbury Rd. NW6—2C 4
Brondesbury Vs. NW6—2C 4
Bronti Clo. SE17—3A 62
Brook Dri. SE11—5D 48

66

Brooke's Ct. EC1—4C 24
Brooke's Mkt. EC1—4D 24
Brooke St. EC1—4C 24
Brook Ga. W1—3C 32
Brook M. N. W2—2D 30
Brook's M. W1—2F 33
Brook St. W1—2F 33
Brook St. W2—2F 31
Brooksville Av. NW6—1A 4
Brown Hart Gdns. W1—2E 33
Browning Clo. W9—2D 18
Browning M. W1—4F 21
Browning St. SE17—2A 62
Brownlow M. WC1—2A 24
Brownlow St. WC1—4B 24
Brown's Arc W1—3B 34
Brown's Bldgs. EC3—6F 27
Brown St. W1—5A 20
Broxwood Way. NW8—1A 8
Brunel Est. W2—5E 17
Brune St. E1—4G 27
Brunswick Centre. WC1—1G 23
Brunswick Clo. Est. EC1—6F 13
Brunswick Ct. SE1—1F 51
Brunswick Gdns. W8—5G 29
Brunswick M. W1—6B 20
Brunswick Pl. N1—6C 14
Brunswick Sq. WC1—1G 23
Brushfield St. E1—4F 27
Bruton La. W1—3H 33
Bruton Pl. W1—3G 33
Bruton St. W1—3G 33
Bryanston M. E. W1—5B 20
Bryanston M. W. W1—5A 20
Bryanston Pl. W1—5A 20
Bryanston Sq. W1—5B 20
Bryanston St. W1—1B 32
Bryant Ct. E2—1H 15
Brydges Pl. WC2—3F 35
Bryer Ct. EC2—3H 25
Buck Hill Wlk. W2—3F to 5F 31
Buckingham Arc. WC2—4G 35
Buckingham Ga. SW1—3H 45 to 4C 46
Buckingham M. SW1—3A 46
Buckingham Pal. Rd. SW1—1F 57
Buckingham Pl. SW1—3A 46
Buckingham St. WC2—4G 35
Buckland St. N1—3D 14
Buckler's All. SW6—6D 52
Bucklersbury. EC4—1B 38
Buckley St. SE1—6C 36
Bucknall St. WC2—6E 23
Budge Row. EC4—1B 38
Budge's Wlk. W2—5B 30
Bulinga St. SW1—1F 59
Bull All. SE1—4E 37
Bull Inn Ct. WC2—3G 35
Bull's Gdns. SW3—6H 43
Bull's Head Pas. SE3—1D 38
Bull Wharf La. EC4—3A 38
Bulmer M. W11—4E 29
Bulmer Pl. W11—4E 29
Bulstrode Pl. W1—5E 21
Bulstrode St. W1—5E 21
Bunhill Row. EC1—1B 26
Bunhouse Pl. SW1—2E 57
Bunyan Ct. EC2—3H 25
Buonaparte M. SW1—2D 58
Burbage Clo. SE1—4C 50
Burdett M. W2—6H 17
Burdett St. SE1—3C 48
Burgess Pk. Ind. Est. SE5—6D 62
Burge St. SE1—5C 50
Burgh St. N1—2G 13
Burgon St. EC4—1F 37
Burleigh St. WC2—2H 35
Burlington Arc. W1—3A 34
Burlington Clo. W9—1D 16
Burlington Gdns. W1—3A 34
Burne St. NW1 SE1—4G 19
Burnsall St. SW3—3H 55
Burrell St. SE1—5F 37
Burrows M. SE1—1E 49
Bursar St. SE1—6E 39
Burton Gro. SE17—3C 62
Burton M. SW1—6F 45
Burton Pl. WC1—6E 11
Burton St. WC1—6E 11

Burwood Pl. W2—6H 19
Bury Ct. EC3—6F 27
Bury Pl. WC1—4F 23
Bury St. EC3—6F 27
Bury St. SW1—4B 34
Bury Wlk. SW3—1G 55
Bush La. EC4—2C 38
Bute St. SW7—6E 43
Butler Pl. SW1—4C 46
Butlers Wharf. SE1—6H 39
Buttesland St. N1—5D 14
Buxton Ct. N1—4A 14
Byng Pl. WC1—2D 22
Byward St. EC3—3F 39
Bywater St. SW3—2A 56
Bywell Pl. W1—5A 22

Cabbell St. NW1—4G 19
Cadiz St. SE17—3A 62
Cadogan Gdns. SW3—6B & 6C 44
Cadogan Ga. SW1—6C 44
Cadogan La. SW1—4D 44
Cadogan Pl. SW1—4C 44
Cadogan Sq. SW1—5B 44
Cadogan St. SW3—1A 56
Cahill St. EC1—2B 26
Caird St. W10—6B 4
Caldew St. SE5—6B 62
Caldwell Yd. EC4—2H 37
Caleb St. SE1—1A 50
Caledonian Rd. N1—4G 11 to 1A 12
Caledonia St. N1—3G 11
Cale St. SW3—2G 55
Callcott St. W8—5E 29
Callendar Rd. SW7—3D 42
Callow St. SW3—4D 54
Calmington Rd. SE5—4F 63
Calshot St. N1—2A 12
Calthorpe St. WC1—1B 24
Calvert Av. E2—6G 15
Calverton. SE17—4D 62
Calvert's Bldgs. SE1—6B 38
Calvin St. E1—2G 27
Camberwell New Rd. SE5—6C 60
Camberwell Rd. SE5—6A 62
Cambourne M. W11—1A 28
Cambridge Av. NW6—2F 5
Cambridge Cir. WC2—1E 35
Cambridge Gdns. NW6—3F 5
Cambridge Gdns. W10—5A 16
Cambridge Ga. NW1—6G 9
Cambridge Ga. M. NW1—6G 9
Cambridge Pl. NW6—4F 5
Cambridge Pl. W8—2A 42
Cambridge Rd. NW6—5F & 4F 5
Cambridge Sq. W2—6G 19
Cambridge St. SW1—1G 57 to 3B 58
Cambridge Ter. NW1—6G 9
Cambridge Ter. M. NW1—6G 9
Cam Ct. SE15—6G 63
Camden High St. NW1—1A 10
Camden Pas. N1—2E 13
Camden St. NW1—1B 10
Camden Wlk. N1—1F 13
Camera Pl. SW10—5D 54
Camlet St. E2—6G 15
Camley St. NW1—1D 10
Camomile St. EC3—5E 27
Campden Gro. W8—1F 41
Campden Hill. W8—1D 40
Campden Hill Gdns. W8—5E 29
Campden Hill Pl. W8—5D 28
Campden Hill Rd. W8—5E 29 to 2F 41
Campden Hill Sq. W8—5D 28
Campden Ho. Clo. W8—1F 41
Campden St. W8—6E 29
Canal St. SE5—5C 62
Candover St. W1—4A 22
Canning Pas. W8—3B 42
(in two parts)
Canning Pl. W8—3B 42
Canning Pl. M. W8—3B 42
Cannon Row. SW1—1F 47
Cannon St. EC4—1H 37 to 2C 38
Canon Murnane Rd. SE1—5G 51
Canon St. N1—1A 14
Canterbury Pl. SE17—1F 61

Canterbury Rd. NW6—3E 5
Canterbury Ter. NW6—3E 5
Canvey St. SE1—5G 37
Capener's Clo. SW1—2C 44
Capland St. NW8—1F & 2F 19
Capper St. WC1—2C 22
Caradoc Clo. W2—6E 17
Carburton St. W1—3H 21
Cardigan St. SE11—2C 60
Cardinal Bourne St. SE1—5C 50
Cardinal Cap All. SE1—4H 37
Cardington St. NW1—5D 10
Carey La. EC2—6H 25
Carey Pl. SW1—1D 58
Carey St. WC2—6B 24
Carlisle Av. EC3—1G 39
Carlisle La. SE1—4B 48
Carlisle M. NW8—3F 19
Carlisle Pl. SW1—5A 46
Carlisle Rd. NW6—1A 4
Carlisle St. W1—6C 22
Carlos Pl. W1—3F 33
Carlow St. NW1—2A 10
Carlton Gdns. SW1—5C 34
Carlton Hill. NW8—3A to 1D 6
Carlton Ho. Ter. SW1—5D 34
Carlton St. SW1—4C 34
Carlton Vale. NW6—3C 4 to 3F 5
Carlyle Sq. SW3—4F 55
Carmarthen Pl. SE1—1E 51
Carmel Ct. W8—1G 41
Carmelite St. EC4—2E 37
Carnaby St. W1—1A 34
Carnegie St. N1—1A 12
Caroline Clo. W2—3H 29
Caroline Gdns. E2—4F 15
Caroline Pl. W2—3H 29
Caroline Pl. M. W2—3H 29
Caroline Ter. SW1—1D 56
Carpenter St. W1—3F 33
Carriage Dri. E. SW11—6D 56
Carriage Dri. N. SW11—6C 56
Carrington St. W1—5G 33
Carroun Rd. SW8—6A 60
Carter Ct. EC4—1F 37
Carteret St. SW1—2D 46
Carter La. EC4—1F 37
Carter Pl. SE17—3A 62
Carter St. SE17—4G 61
Carthusian St. EC1—3G 25
Carting La. WC2—3H 35
Cartwright Gdns. WC1—6F 11
Castellain Mans. W9—6H 5
Castellain Rd. W9—6H 5
Castle Baynard St. EC4—2G 37
Castle Ct. EC3—1D 38
Castle Ind. Est. SE17—5H 49
Castle La. SW1—3B 46
Castlereagh St. W1—6A 20
Castletown Rd. W14—3A 52
Castle Yd. SE1—4F 37
Catesby St. SE17—1C 62
Cathcart Rd. SW10—5A 54
Cathedral Piazza. SW1—4A 46
Cathedral Pl. EC4—6G 25
Cathedral St. SE1—5B 38
Catherine Pl. SW1—3A 46
Catherine St. WC2—2H 35
Catherine Wheel All. E1—4F 27
Catherine Wheel Yd. SW1—6A 34
Cator St. SE15—6H 63
Cato St. W1—5H 19
Catton St. WC1—5H 23
Causton St. SW1—1D 58
Cavaye Pl. SW10—4D 54
Cavendish Av. NW8—3E 7
Cavendish Clo. NW8—4F 7
Cavendish Ct. EC3—5F 27
Cavendish M. N. W1—4H 21
Cavendish M. S. W1—4H 21
Cavendish Pl. W1—5H 21
Cavendish Sq. W1—5G 21
Cavendish St. N1—3B 14
Caversham M. SW3—4B 56
Caversham St. SW3—4A 56
Caxton St. SW1—3C 46
Caxton Wlk. WC2—1E 35
Cayton Pl. EC1—5B 14

67

Cayton St. EC1—5B 14
Cecil Ct. WC2—3E 35
Celbridge M. W2—5H 17
Centaur St. SE1—3B 48
Central St. EC1—5H 13
Centre Ct. W2—3B 30
Cervantes Ct. W2—1A 30
Chadwell St. EC1—4D 12
Chadwick St. SW1—4D 46
Chagford St. NW1—2B 20
Chalbury Wlk. N1—2B 12
Chaldon Rd. SW6—6A 52
Challoner Cres. W14—3C 52
Challoner St. W14—3B 52
Chalmers Wlk. SE17—6H 61
Chalton St. NW1—2C 10
Chambord St. E2—5H 15
Chancel St. SE1—5F 37
Chancery La. WC2—5B 24
Chance St.—1G 27
  E1 1-5 & 2-6
  E2 remainder
Chandos Pl. WC2—3F 35
Chandos St. W1—5G 21
Change All. EC3—1C 38
Chantry St. N1—1G 13
Chapel Ct. SE1—1B 50
Chapel Mkt. N1—2C 12
Chapel Pl. N1—2D 12
Chapel Pl. W1—6G 21
Chapel Side. W2—3G 29
Chapel St. NW1—4G 19
Chapel St. SW1—3E 45
Chaplin Clo. SE1—1E 49
Chapone Pl. W1—1D 34
Chapter Ho. Ct. EC4—6G 25
Chapter Rd. SE17—4G 61
Chapter St. SW1—1D 58
Chapter Ter. W14—4F 61
Charfield Ct. W9—3H 17
Charing Cross. SW1—5E 35
Charing Cross Rd. WC2—6D 22 to 3E 35
Charlbert St. NW8—2G 7
Charles La. NW8—3F 7
Charles Pl. NW1—6B 10
Charles II St. SW1—4C to 4D 34
Charles Sq. N1—5D 14
Charles St. W1—5F 33
Charleston St. SE17—1A 62
Charleville Rd. W14—3A 52
Charlotte M. W1—3B 22
Charlotte Pl. SW1—6A 46
Charlotte Pl. W1—4B 22
Charlotte Rd. EC2—6E 15
Charlotte St. W1—3B 22
Charlotte Ter. N1—1B 12
Charlton Pl. N1—2E 13
Charlwood Pl. SW1—1B 58
Charlwood St. SW1—3A 58
Char ing Cross Underground Shopping
                Concourse. WC2—3F 35
Charrington St. NW1—2C 10
Charterhouse Bldgs. EC1—2G 25
Charterhouse M. EC1—3G 25
Charterhouse Sq. EC1—3G 25
Charterhouse St. EC1—4E 25
Charteris Rd. NW6—1D 4
Chart St. N1—5C 14
Chatham St. SE17—6C 50
Cheapside. EC2—6H 25
Cheesemans Ter. W14—3C & 4B 52
Chelsea Bri. SW1 & SW8—4F 57
Chelsea Bri. Rd. SW1—2D 56
Chelsea Embkmt. SW3—6G 55 to 4F 57
Chelsea Mnr. Gdns. SW3—4H 55
Chelsea Mnr. St. SW3—3H 55
Chelsea Pk. Gdns. SW3—5E 55
Chelsea Sq. SW3—3F 55
Cheltenham Ter. SW3—2B 56
Cheney Rd. N1—3F 11
Chenies M. WC1—2C 22
Chenies Pl. NW1—2D 10
Chenies St. WC1—3C 22
Cheniston Gdns. W8—3G 41
Chepstow Cres. W11—2E 29
Chepstow Pl. W2—1F 29
Chepstow Rd. W2—5F 17
Chepstow Vs. W11—2D 28

Chequer St. EC1—2A 26
Cherbury St. N1—3C 14
Cherry Tree Wlk. EC1—2B 26
Chesham Clo. SW1—4D 44
Chesham M. SW1—4D 44
Chesham Pl. SW1—4D 44
Chesham St. SW1—4D 44
Chesson Rd. W14—5B 52
Chester Clo. SW1—3F 45
Chester Clo. N. NW1—4G 9
Chester Clo. S. NW1—4G 9
Chester Cotts. SW1—1D 56
Chester Ct. NW1—4G 9
Chesterfield Gdns. W1—5F 33
Chesterfield Hill. W1—4F 33
Chesterfield St. W1—5F 33
Chester Ga. NW1—6G 9
Chester M. SW1—3F 45
Chester Pl. NW1—4G 9
Chester Rd. NW1—6E 9
Chester Row. SW1—1D 56
Chester Sq. SW1—5F 45
Chester Sq. M. SW1—5G 45
Chester St. SW1—3F 45
Chester Ter. NW1—4G 9
Chesterton Rd. W10—4A 16
Chesterton Sq. W8—6D 40
Chester Way. SE11—1D 60
Chestnut All. SW6—5D 52
Chestnut Ct. SW6—5D 52
Chettle Clo. SE1—4C 50
Cheval Pl. SW7—4H 43
Cheyne Gdns. SW3—5A 56
Cheyne M. SW3—5H 55
Cheyne Pl. SW3—5B 56
Cheyne Row. SW3—5G 55
Cheyne Wlk. SW3—6G 55 to 5A 56
Cheyne Wlk. SW10—6F 55
Chichele St. SE1—1A 48
Chichester Bldgs. SE1—5E 51
Chichester Rents. WC2—6C 24
Chichester Rd. NW6—3E 5
Chichester Rd. W2—4A 18
Chichester St. SW1—3B 58
Childs Pl. SW5—1G 53
Childs St. SW5—6G 41
Child's Wlk. SW5—6G 41
Chiltern St. W1—3C 20
Chilworth M. W2—6D 18
Chilworth St. W2—1C 30
Chippenham Gdns. NW6—6E 5
Chippenham M. W9—2E 17
Chippenham Rd. W9—6E 5
Chiswell St. EC1—3B 26
Chitty St. W1—3B 22
Christchurch St. SW3—4A 56
Christchurch Ter. SW3—4A 56
Christina St. EC2—1E 27
Christopher Pl. NW1—5D 10
Christophers M. W11—5A 28
Christopher St. EC2—3D 26
Chumleigh St. SE5—4E 63
Church Cloisters. EC3—3E 39
Church Entry. EC4—1F 37
Churchill Gdns. SW1—4A 58
Churchill Gdns. Rd. SW1—4H 57
Church Pl. SW1—4B 34
Church St:—3E 19
  NW8 1-127 & 2-142
  W2 remainder
Church St. Est. NW8—2F 19
Churchway. NW1—5D 10
Churchyard Row. SE11—6F 49
Churton Pl. SW1—1B 58
Churton St. SW1—1B 58
Circus M. W1—4A 20
Circus Pl. EC2—5D 26
Circus Rd. NW8—4D 6
Cirencester St. W2—3G 17
City Garden Row. N1—3G 13
City Rd. EC1—3E 13 to 2C 26
Clabon M. SW1—5B 44
Clanricarde Gdns. W2—3G 29
Clare Gdns. W11—1B 28
Clare Mkt. WC2—1A 36
Claremont Clo. N1—4D 12
Claremont Rd. W9—3B 4

Claremont Sq. N1—3C 12
Clarence Gdns. NW1—6H 9
Clarence Ga. Gdns. NW1—2B 20
Clarence Pas. NW1—3F 11
Clarence Ter. NW1—1B 20
Clarence Yd. SE17—2H 61
Clarendon Clo. W2—2G 31
Clarendon Cross. W11—4A 28
Clarendon Gdns. W9—2C 18
Clarendon Gro. NW1—4D 10
Clarendon M. W2—1G 31
Clarendon Pl. W2—2G 31
Clarendon Rd. W11—2A 28
Clarendon St. SW1—3H 57
Clarendon Ter. W9—1D 18
Clareville Gro. SW7—1D 54
Clareville St. SW7—1C 54
Clarges M. W1—5G 33
Clarges St. W1—5G 33
Clarke's M. W1—4F 21
Clarkson Row. NW1—3H 9
Clark's Pas. SW8—5G 59
Clark's Pl. EC2—6E 27
Claverton St. SW1—3B 58
Claylands Pl. SW8—6B 60
Claylands Rd. SW8—6B 60
Clay St. W1—4C 20
Clayton St. SE11—5C 60
Clearwell Dri. W9—2H 17
Cleaver Sq. SE11—3D 60
Cleaver St. SE11—2D 60
Clem Attlee Ct. SW6—6C 52
Clement's Inn. WC2—1B 36
Clement's Inn Pas. WC2—1A 36
Clement's La. EC4—2D 38
Clennam St. SE1—1A 50
Clenston M. W1—6B 20
Clere Pl. EC2—1D 26
Clere St. EC2—1D 26
Clerkenwell Clo. EC1—1E 25
Clerkenwell Grn. EC1—2E 25
Clerkenwell Rd. EC1—3C 24
Cleveland M. W1—3A 22
Cleveland Pl. SW1—5B 34
Cleveland Row. SW1—6A 34
Cleveland Sq. W2—1B 30
Cleveland St. W1—2H 21
Cleveland Ter. W2—6C 18
Clifford's Inn Pas. EC4—1C 36
Clifford St. W1—3H 33
Clifton Ct. W9—1D 18
Clifton Gdns. W9—2B 18
Clifton Hill. NW6 & NW8—2A to 1C 6
Clifton Pl. W2—1F 31
Clifton Rd. W9—1C 18
Clifton St. EC2—3D 26
Clifton Vs. W9—3E 17
Clinger Ct. N1—1E 15
Clink St. SE1—4B 38
Clipstone M. W1—3A 22
Clipstone St. W1—3H 21
Clive Ct. W9—6C 6
Cliveden Pl. SW1—6D 44
Cloak La. EC4—2B 38
Clock Tower. M. N1—1A 14
Cloisters, The. E1—3G 27
Cloth Ct. EC1—4G 25
Cloth Fair. EC1—4G 25
Cloth St. EC1—4H 25
Cloudesley Pl. N1—1D 12
Cloudesley Rd. N1—1C 12
Cloudesley St. N1—1D 12
Clover M. SW3—5B 56
Club Row.—6H 15
  E1 1-11 & 2-10
  E2 remainder
Clunbury St. N1—3D 14
Cluny Est. SE1—3E 51
Cluny M. SW5—1E 53
Cluny Pl. SE1—3E 51
Clydesdale Rd. W11—6C 16
Coach & Horses Yd. W1—2H 33
Cobb's Ct. EC4—1F 37
Cobb St. E1—5G 27
Coburg Rd. SE5—5G 63
Cobourg St. NW1—6B 10
Coburg Clo. SW1—5B 46
Cochrane Clo. NW8—3F 7

Cutlers Gdns. E1—3F 27
Cutler St. E1—6F 27
Cut, The. SE1—6E 37
Cygnet St. E1—1H 27
Cynthia St. N1—3B 12
Cypress Pl. W1—2B 22
Cyrus St. EC1—1F 25

Dacre St. SW1—3D 46
Dain Ct. W8—5G 41
Dale Rd. SE17—6G 61
Dale Row. W11—1A 28
Dallington St. EC1—1F 25
Dame St. N1—2H 13
Danbury St. N1—2G 13
Danesfield. SE17—4E 63
Dane St. WC1—4H 23
Daniel Gdns. SE15—6H 63
Dansey Pl. W1—2D 34
Dante Pl. SE11—6F 49
Dante Rd. SE11—6F 49
Danube St. SW3—2H 55
Danvers St. SW3—5F 55
D'Arblay St. W1—1B 34
Dartford St. SE17—4A 62
Dartmouth Clo. W11—5D 16
Dartmouth St. SW1—2D 46
Dart St. W10—5B 4
Darwin St. SE17—6C 50
  (in two parts)
Date St. SE17—3B 62
Daventry St. NW1—3G 19
Davey's Ct. WC2—3F 35
Davey St. SE15—6H 63
Davidge St. SE1—2F 49
David M. W1—3C 20
Davies M. W1—2F 33
Davies St. W1—1F 33
Dawes St. SE17—2C 62
Dawson Pl. W2—2E 29
Deacon Way. SE17—6H 49
Dean Bradley St. SW1—5F 47
Deanery M. W1—5E 33
Deanery St. W1—5E 33
Dean Farrar St. SW1—3D 46
Dean Ryle St. SW1—5F 47
Dean's Bldgs. SE17—1C 62
Deans Ct. EC4—1G 37
Dean's M. W1—5G 21
Dean's Pl. SW1—1C 58
Dean Stanley St. SW1—4F 97
Dean St. W1—6C 22
Dean's Yd. SW1—3E 47
Dean Trench St. SW1—5F 47
Decima St. SE1—3E 51
Defoe Ho. EC2—3H 25
Delaford St. SW6—6B 52
Delamere Ter. W2—3A 18
Delancey Pas. NW1—1H 9
Delancey St. NW1—1G 9
De Laune St. SE17—4E 61
Delaware Mans. W9—1G 17
Delaware Rd. W9—1G 17
Dell's M. SW1—1B 58
Delverton Rd. SE17—3G 61
Denbigh Clo. W11—2D 28
Denbigh M. SW1—1A 58
Denbigh Pl. SW1—2A 58
Denbigh Rd. W11—2D 28
Denbigh St. SW1—1B 58
DenbighTer. W11—2D 28
Denby Ct. SE11—4H 33
Denholme Rd. W9—5D 4
Denman St. W1—3C 34
Denmark Pl. WC2—6E 23
Denmark Rd. NW6—3D 4 & 3E 5
Denmark St. WC2—6E 23
Denning Clo. NW8—5D 6
Denny Cres. SE11—2D 60
Denny St. SE11—2D 60
Denyer St. SW3—6A 44
Depot St. SE5—6B 62
Derby Ga. SW1—1F 47
Derby St. W1—5F 33
Dereham Pl. EC2—6F 15
Dering St. W1—1G 33
Dering Yd. W1—1G 33

Derry St. W8—2H 41
De Vere Gdns. W8—2B 42
Deverell St. SE1—4B 50
De Vere M. W8—3B 42
Devereux Ct. WC2—1C 36
Devizes St. N1—1C 14
Devonia Rd. N1—2F 13
Devonshire Clo. W1—3G 21
Devonshire M. N. W1—3F 21
Devonshire M. S. W1—3F 21
Devonshire M. W. W1—2F 21
Devonshire Pl. W1—2E 21
Devonshire Pl. M. W1—3E 21
Devonshire Row. EC2—5F 27
Devonshire Row. M. W1—3G 21
Devonshire Sq. E1—5F 27
Devonshire Sq. EC2—5F 27
Devonshire St. W1—3E to 3H 21
Devonshire Ter. W2—1C 30
De Walden St. W1—4E 21
Dewey Rd. N1—2C 12
Diadem Ct. W1—6C 22
Dial Wlk., The. W8—1A 42
Diana Pl. NW1—1H 21
Dibdin Row. SE1—3D 48
Dickens Sq. SE1—3A 50
Dighton Ct. SE5—5H 61
Dignum St. N1—2C 12
  (in three parts)
Dilke St. SW3—5B 56
Dingley Pl. EC1—5A 14
Dingley Rd. EC1—5H 13
Disbrowe Rd. W6—6A 52
Disney Pl. SE1—1A 50
Disney St. SE1—1A 50
Diss St. E2—4H 15
Distaff La. EC4—2H 37
Distin St. SE11—6C 48
Doby Ct. EC4—2A 38
Doddington Gro. SE17—4F 61
Doddington Pl. SE17—4E 61
Dodson St. SE1—2D 48
Dog & Duck Yd. WC1—4A 24
Dolben St. SE1—6F 37
  (in two parts)
Dolland St. SE11—3B 60
Dolphin Sq. SW1—4C 58
Dombey St. WC1—3H 23
Domingo St. EC1—2H 25
Dominion St. EC2—4D 26
Domville Gro. SE5—3G 63
Donaldson Rd. NW6—1C 4
Donegal St. N1—3B 12
Donne Pl. SW3—6H 43
Doon St. SE1—5C 36
Doric Way. NW1—5D 10
Dorrington St. EC1—4C 24
Dorrit St. SE1—1A 50
Dorset Bldgs. EC4—1E 37
Dorset Clo. NW1—3B 20
Dorset M. SW1—3G 45
Dorset Rise. EC4—1E 37
Dorset Sq. NW1—2B 20
Dorset St. W1—4C 20
Doughty M. WC1—2A 24
Doughty St. WC1—1A 24
Douglas St. SW1—1C 58
Dourdan Ct. EC1—4D 24
Douro Pl. W8—3A 42
Dove Ct. EC2—1B 38
Dovehouse St. SW3—2F 55
Dove M. SW5—1C 54
Dover St. W1—4H 33
Dover Yd. W1—4H 33
Dove Wlk. SW1—2D 56
Dowend Ct. SE15—6G 63
Dowgate Hill. EC4—2B 38
Dowland St. W10—4B 4
Downfield Clo. W9—2G 17
Downing St. SW1—1F 47
Down St. W1—6F 33
Down St. M. W1—6F 33
Doyce St. SE1—1H 49
D'Oyley St. SW1—6D 44
Draco St. SE17—4H 61
Dragon Yd. WC1—5G 23
Drake St. WC1—4H 23
Draper's Gdns. EC2—5C 26

Draycott Av. SW3—6H 43
Draycott Pl. SW3—1B 56
Draycott Ter. SW3—6B 44
Drayford Clo. W9—1C 16
Drayson M. W8—2G 41
Drayton Gdns. SW10—2C 54
Droop St. W10—6A 4
Druid St. SE1—1F to 3H 51
Drummond Cres. NW1—5C 10
Drummond Ga. SW1—2D 58
Drummond St. NW1—6A to 6C 10
Drury La. WC2—6G 23
Dryden Ct. SE11—6E 49
Dryden St. WC2—1G 35
Drysdale Pl. N1—5F 15
Drysdale St. N1—5F 15
Ducal St. E2—6H 15
Duchess M. W1—4G 21
Duchess of Bedford's Wlk. W8—2D 40
Duchess St. W1—4G 21
Duchy Pl. SE1—5D 36
Duchy St. SE1—4D 36
Duck La. W1—1C 34
Dudley Rd. NW6—2B 4
Dudley St. W2—4D 18
Dudmaston M. SW3—2F 55
Dufferin Av. EC1—2B 26
Dufferin St. EC1—2A 26
Dufour's Pl. W1—1B 34
Duke of Wellington Pl. SW1—1F 45
Duke of York St. SW1—4C 34
Duke's La. W8—1G 41
Duke's M. W1—6E 21
Duke's Pl. EC3—6G 27
Duke's Rd. WC1—6E 11
Duke St. W1—6E 21 to 2F 33
Duke St. Hill. SE1—5C 38
Duke St. Saint James's. SW1—4B 34
Duke's Yd. W1—2F 33
Duncannon St. WC2—4F 35
Duncan St. N1—2E 13
Duncan Ter. N1—3E & 1F 13
Dunloe St. E2—4G 15
Dunn's Pas. WC1—5G 23
Dunraven St. W1—2C 32
Dunstable M. W1—3E 21
Dunster Ct. EC3—2F 39
Dunstersville Way. SE1—2D 50
Dunston Rd. E8—1H 15
Dunton Rd. SE1—2G 63
Dunworth M. W11—6C 16
Duplex Ride. SW1—2C 44
Durham Ho. St. WC2—3G 35
Durham St. SW3—3B 56
Durham St. SE11—4A 60
Durham Ter. W2—6G 17
Dursley Ct. SE15—6F 63
Durweston M. W1—4C 20
Durweston St. W1—4B 20
Dyer's Bldgs. EC1—5C 24
Dymock Ct. SE15—6F 63
Dyott St. WC1—5E 23
Dysart St. EC2—2D 26

Eagle Ct. EC1—3F 25
Eagle Pl. SW1—4C 34
Eagle St. WC1—4A 24
Eagle Wharf Rd. N1—2A 14
Eamont St. NW8—2G 7
Eardley Cres. SW5—3F 53
Earlham St. WC2—1E & 1F 35
Earl Rd. SE1—2G 63
Earl's Ct. Gdns. SW5—1G 53
Earl's Ct. Sq. SW5—2G 53
Earl's Ct. Rd.—4E 41 to 2H 53
  W8 1-109 & 2-138
  SW5 remainder
Earls Ter. W8—4D 40
Earlstoke St. EC1—5F 13
Earl St. EC2—3D 26
Earls Wlk. W8—5E 41
Earnshaw St. WC2—6E 23
Earsby St. W14—5A 40
Easley's M. W1—6F 21
Eastbourne Bldgs. SE1—4E 51
Eastbourne M. W2—6C 18
Eastbourne Ter. W2—5C 18

70

Eastcastle St. W1—6A 22
Eastcheap. EC3—2D 38
E. Harding St. EC4—6D 24
Easton St. WC1—6C 12
East Pas. EC1—4G 25
E. Poultry Av. EC1—4F 25
East Rd. N1—5C 14
East Row. W10—2A 16
E. Smithfield. E1—3H 39
East St. SE17—3A 62 to 1F 63
Eaton Clo. SW1—6D 44
Eaton Ga. SW1—6D 44
Eaton La. SW1—4G 45
Eaton M. N. SW1—5E 45
Eaton M. S. SW1—5F 45
Eaton M. W. SW1—6E 45
Eaton Pl. SW1—5D 44
Eaton Row. SW1—5E 45
Eaton Sq. SW1—6D 44 to 4F 45
Eaton Ter. SW1—6D 44
Eaton Ter. M. SW1—5D 44
Ebbisham Dri. SW8—5A 60
Ebenezer St. N1—5B 14
Ebley Clo. SE15—6G 63
Ebor St. E1—1G 27
Ebury Bri. SW1—2F 57
Ebury Bri. Est. SW1—2F 57
Ebury Bri. Rd. SW1—3F 57
Ebury M. SW1—6F 45
Ebury M. E. SW1—5F 45
Ebury Sq. SW1—1F 57
Ebury St. SW1—1E 57 to 4G 45
Eccleston Bri. SW1—6G 45
Eccleston M. SW1—4E 45
Eccleston Pl. SW1—6G & 5G 45
Eccleston Sq. SW1—1H 57
Eccleston Sq. M. SW1—1H 57
Eccleston St. SW1—5F 45
Eckford St. N1—2B 12
Edbrooke Rd. W9—2F 17
Eden Clo. W8—3F 41
Edenham Way. W10—3C 16
Edge St. W8—5F 9
Edgware Rd. W2—2D 18 to 1B 32
Edinburgh Ga. SW1—1B 44
Edith Gro. SW10—5B 54
Edith Rd. W14—1A 52
Edith Ter. SW10—6B 54
Edith Vs. W14—1B 52
Edward Edward's Ho. SE1—5F 37
Edwardes Sq. W8—4D 40
Edward M. NW1—4G 9
Edwards M. W1—1D 32
Edwards M. Gdns. W1—6E 21
Edward Sq. N1—1H 11
Egerton Cres. SW3—5H 43
Egerton Gdns. SW3—5H 43
Egerton Gdns. M. SW3—4H 43
Egerton Pl. SW3—5H 43
Egerton Ter. SW3—4H 43
Elba Pl. SE17—6B 50
Elder St. E1—3G 27
Eldon Rd. W8—4A 42
Eldon St. EC2—4D 26
Elephant & Castle. SE1—6G 49
Elephant Rd. SE17—6H 49
Elgin Av. W9—2D 16 to 5A 6
Elgin Ct. W9—6G 5
Elgin Cres. W11—3A to 1C 28
Elgin M. W11—6A 16
Elgin M. N. W9—5A 6
Elgin M. S. W9—5A 6
Elia M. N1—3F 13
Elias Pl. SW8—6C 60
Elia St. N1—3F 13
Elim Est. SE1—3D 50
Elim St. SE1—3D 50
(in two parts)
Elizabeth Bri. SW1—1G 57
Elizabeth Clo. W9—1C 18
Elizabeth Ct. SW1—4D 46
Elizabeth Newcomen Ho. SE1—1C 50
Elizabeth St. SW1—6E 45
Elkington Point. SE11—1C 60
Elkstone St. SE15—6E 63
Elkstone Rd. W10—3B 16
Elliott's Ct. EC4—6F 25

Elliott's Pl. N1—1F 13
Elliott's Row. SE11—5F 49
Ellis St. SW1—6C 44
Ellwood Ct. SW7—2H 17
Elm Ct. EC4—1C 36
Elm Pk. Gdns. SW10—4E 55
Elm Pk. La. SW3—4D 54
Elm Pk. Mans. SW10—5D 54
Elm Pk. Rd. SW3—5D 54
Elm Pl. SW7—2E 55
Elm Quay Ct. SW8—5D 58
Elms M. W2—2D 30
Elm St. WC1—2B 24
Elm Tree Clo. NW8—5E 7
Elm Tree Rd. NW8—4E 7
Elnathan M. W9—2H 17
Elsham Rd. W14—3A 40
Elsted St. SE17—1D 62
Elvaston M. SW7—4C 42
Elvaston Pl. SW7—4B 42
Elverton St. SW1—5C 46
Ely Ct. EC1—4D 24
Ely Pl. EC1—4D 24
Elystan Pl. SW3—2A 56
Elystan St. SW3—1G 55
Elystan Wlk. N1—1C 12
Embankment Gdns. SW3—5C 56
Embankment Pl. WC2—5G 35
Embassy Ct. NW8—3F 7
Emberton. SE17—4E 63
Emerald St. WC1—3A 24
Emerson St. SE1—4H 37
Emery Hill St. SW1—5B 46
Emery St. SE1—3D 48
Emperor's Ga. SW7—5A 42
Empress Pl. SW6—4F 53
Empress St. SE17—4A 62
Enbrook St. W10—6A 4
Endell St. WC2—6F 23
Endsleigh Gdns. WC1—1C 22
Endsleigh Pl. WC1—1C 22
Endsleigh St. WC1—6D 10
Enford St. W1—3A 20
Engine Ct. SW1—6B 34
English Grounds. SE1—5E 39
Ennismore Gdns. SW7—3G 43
Ennismore Gdns. M. SW7—3F 43
Ennismore M. SW7—3G 43
Ennismore St. SW7—3G 43
Ensor M. SW7—2D 54
Epworth St. EC2—2C 26
Erasmus St. SW1—1E 59
Errington Rd. W9—1D 16
Errol St. EC1—2A 26
Esmond Rd. NW6—1C 4
Essendine Rd. W9—6F 5
Essex Ct. EC4—1C 36
Essex Rd. N1—1F 13
Essex St. WC2—1B 36
Essex Vs. W8—3E 41
Esterbrooke St. SW1—1D 58
Ethel St. SE17—1A 62
Europa Pl. EC1—6H 13
Eustace Rd. SW6—6E 53
Euston Gro. NW1—6D 10
Euston Rd. NW1—2H 21 to 4G 11
Euston Sq. NW1—6C 10
Euston Sta. Colonnade. NW1—6C 10
Euston St. NW1—6B 10
Evelyn Gdns. SW7—3D 54
Evelyn Wlk. N1—3C 14
Evelyn Yd. W1—5D 22
Eversholt St. NW1—2A 10
Everton Bldgs. NW1—5A 10
Ewer St. SE1—5G 37
Excel Ct. WC2—4D 34
Exchange Ct. WC2—3G 35
Exchange Pl. EC2—3E 27
Exchange Sq. EC2—3F 27
Exeter St. WC2—2H 35
Exhibition Rd. SW7—2E 43
Exmouth Mkt. EC1—1C 24
Exmouth M. NW1—6B 10
Exon St. SE17—1E 63
Exton St. SE1—6C 36
Eyre Ct. NW8—2D 6
Eyre St. Hill. EC1—2C 24

Fairchild Pl. EC2—2F 27
Fairchild St. EC2—2F 27
Fairholme Rd. W14—3B 52
Fairholt St. SW7—3H 43
Fairlop Pl. NW8—5F 7
Fair St. SE1—6F 39
Falconberg Ct. W1—6D 22
Falconberg M. W1—6D 22
Falcon Clo. SE1—5G 37
Falcon Ct. EC4—1D 36
Falcon Ct. N1—4G 13
Falkirk St. N1—4F 15
Falmouth Ho. SE11—2E 61
Falmouth Rd. SE1—5A 50
Fane St. W14—4C 52
Fann St. EC1—3H 25
Fanshaw St. N1—4E 15
Fareham St. W1—6C 22
Farmer St. W8—4F 29
Farm La. SW6—6F 53
Farm Pl. W8—5E 29
Farm St. W1—4F 33
Farnell M. SW5—2G 53
Farnham Pl. SE1—5G 37
Farnham Royal. SE11—3A 60
Farringdon La. EC1—2D 24
Farringdon Rd. EC1—1C 24
Farringdon St. EC4—5E 25
Fashion St. E1—4H 27
Faulkner's All. EC1—3E 25
Faunce St. SE17—4E 61
Fawcett St. SW10—5A 54
Featherstone St. EC1—1B 26
Fellows Ct. E2—3H 15
Fenchurch Av. EC3—1E 39
Fenchurch Bldgs. EC3—1F 39
Fenchurch Pl. EC3—2F 39
Fenchurch St. EC3—2D 38
Fen Ct. EC3—1E 39
Fendall St. SE1—4G & 3G 51
Fenelon Pl. W14—1D 52
Fenning St. SE1—1D 50
Fentiman Rd. SW8—6G 59
Fermoy Rd. W9—2C 16
Fernhead Rd. W9—4C 4
Fernsbury St. WC1—5C 12
Fernshaw Rd. SW10—6B 54
Fetter La. EC4—6D 24
Field Ct. WC1—4B 24
Fielding St. SE17—4H 61
Field St. WC1—4H 11
Fife Ter. N1—2A 12
Filton St. SE15—6E 63
Finborough Rd. SW10—3G 53
Finch La. EC3—1D 38
Finchley Pl. NW8—2D 6
Finchley Rd. NW8—1D 6
Finck St. SE1—2B 48
Finsbury Av. EC2—4D 26
Finsbury Av. Sq. EC2—4D 26
Finsbury Cir. EC2—4C 26
Finsbury Est. EC1—6E 13
Finsbury Mkt. EC2—3E 27
(in two parts)
Finsbury Pavement. EC2—4C 26
Finsbury Sq. EC2—3C 26
Finsbury St. EC2—3C 26
First Av. W10—1B 16
First St. SW3—5H 43
Fisher St. WC1—4H 23
Fisherton St. NW8—1E 19
Fish St. Hill. EC3—3D 38
Fitzalan St. SE11—5B 48
Fitzgeorge Av. W14—1A 52
Fitzhardinge St. W1—6D 20
Fitzjames Av. W14—1A 52
Fitzmaurice Pl. W1—4G 33
Fitzroy M. W1—2A 22
Fitzroy Sq. W1—2A 22
Fitzroy St. W1—2A 22
(in two parts)
Flaxman Ct. W1—1C 34
Flaxman Ter. WC1—6E 11
Fleet La. EC4—6E 25
Fleet Sq. WC1—4A 12
Fleet St. EC4—1C 36
Fleming Ct. W2—4E 19
Fleming Rd. SE17—5F 61

Fleur-de-Lis Ct. EC4—6D 24
Fleur-de-Lis St. E1—2G 27
Flinton St. SE17—2F 63
Flint St. SE17—1C 62
Flitcroft St. WC2—1E 35
Flood St. SW3—3H 55
Flood Wlk. SW3—4H 55
Floral St. WC2—2F 35
Florence Ct. W9—6C 6
Flower & Dean Wlk. E1—4H 27
Flower Wlk., The. SW7—1C 42
Foley St. W1—4A 22
Folgate St. E1—3F 27
Follingham Ct. N1—5F 15
Folly M. W11—6B 16
Fontenoy Pas. SE11—1F 61
Fordingley Rd. W9—5D 4
Fore St. EC2—4A 26
Fore St. Av. EC2—4B 26
Formosa St. W9—3A to 2B 18
Forset St. W1—6A 20
Forston St. N1—2B 14
Forsyth Gdns. SE17—5F 61
Fort St. E1—4F 27
Fortune St. EC1—2A 26
Fosbury M. W2—3A 30
Foscote M. W9—3F 17
Foster La. EC2—6H 25
Foubert's Pl. W1—1A 34
Foulis Ter. SW7—2E 55
Founders Ct. EC2—6C 26
Foundry M. NW1—6B 10
Fountain Ct. EC4—2C 36
Fournier St. E1—4H 27
Fourth Av. W10—1A 16
Foxcote. SE17—3F 63
Fox & Knot St. EC1—3G 25
Frampton St. NW8—2E 19
Francis Ct. E1—3F 25
Francis St. SW1—3A 46
Frankland Rd. SW7—4D 42
Franklin Sq. W14—4D 52
Franklin's Row. SW3—2C 56
Frazier St. SE1—2C 48
Frederick Clo. W2—2A 32
Frederick Rd. SE17—4G 61
Frederick's Pl. EC2—1B 38
Frederick's Row. EC1—4F 13
Frederick St. WC1—5H 11
Frederic M. SW1—2C 44
Fremantle St. SE17—2E 63
French Ordinary Ct. EC3—2F 39
French Pl. E1—6F 15
Friars Clo. SE1—5F 37
Friar St. EC4—1F 37
Friary Ct. SW1—6B 34
Friday St. EC4—1H 37
Friend St. EC1—4E 13
Frith St. W1—1D 34
Frome St. N1—2H 13
Frye's Bldgs. N1—5D 12
Frying Pan All. E1—4G 27
Ftzroy Ct. W1—2B 22
Fulham Rd.—6A 54 to 1G 55
  SW3 77-267 & 44-132
  SW10 remainder
Fullwood's M. N1—4D 14
Fulton M. W2—2B 30
Fulwood Pl. WC1—4B 24
Furnival St. EC4—5C 24
Fynes St. SW1—6D 46

Gabriel's Wharf. SE1—4C 36
Gage St. WC1—3H 23
Gainsford St. SE1—6G 39
Galway St. EC1—6A 14
Gambia St. SE1—6F 37
Ganton St. W1—2A 34
Garbutt Pl. W1—4E 21
Garden Ct. EC4—2C 36
Garden M. W2—3F 29
Garden Rd. NW8—4D 6
Garden Row. SE1—4F 49
Garden Ter. SW1—2C 58
Garden Ter. SW7—2H 43
Garden Wlk. EC2—6E 15
Gardners La. EC4—2H 37

Gard St. EC1—5G 13
Garlick Hill. EC4—2A 38
Garnault M. EC1—6D 12
Garnault Pl. EC1—6D 12
Garrett St. EC1—1A 26
Garrick St. WC2—2F 35
Garrick Yd. WC2—2F 35
Garway Rd. W2—1G 29
Gascoigne Pl. E2—5H 15
Gasholder Pl. SE11—3B 60
Gaspar Clo. SW5—6A 42
Gaspar M. SW5—6A 42
Gateforth St. NW8—2G 19
Gate M. SW7—2H 43
Gatesborough St. EC2—1E 27
Gate St. WC2—5H 23
Gateway. SE17—4A 62
Gateways, The. SW3—1A 56
Gatliff Rd. SW1—3F 57
Gaunt St. SE1—3G 49
Gavel St. SE17—6D 50
Gayfere St. SW1—4F 47
Gaywood St. SE1—4F 49
Gaza St. SE17—3F 61
Gedling St. SE1—3H 51
Gees Ct. W1—1F 33
Gee St. EC1—1G 25
Geffrye Ct. N1—3F 15
Geffrye St. E2—2G 15
George & Catherine Wheel All. EC2
                              —4F 27
George Ct. WC2—3G 35
George Inn Yd. SE1—6C 38
George M. NW1—6B 10
George St. W1—6A 20
George Yd. EC3—1D 38
George Yd. W1—2E 33
Georgina Gdns. E2—5H 15
Geraldine St. SE11—4F 49
Gerald M. SW1—6F 45
Gerald Rd. SW1—6E 45
Gerrard Pl. W1—2E 35
Gerrard Rd. N1—2F 13
Gerrard St. W1—2D 34
Gerridge St. SE1—3D 48
Gertrude St. SW10—6C 54
Gibbon's Rents. SE1—6E 39
Gibbs Grn. W14—3C 52
Gibson Rd. SE11—1A 60
Gilbert Pl. WC1—4F 23
Gilbert Pl. WC1—5F 23
Gilbert Rd. SE11—1D 60
Gilbert St. W1—1F 33
Gildea St. W1—4H 21
Gillingham M. SW1—6H 45
Gillingham Row. SW1—6A 46
Gillingham St. SW1—6H 45
Gilston Rd. SW10—3C 54
Giltspur St. EC1—5F 25
Gladstone St. SE1—4E 49
Glasgow Ter. SW1—3A 58
Glasshill St. SE1—1G 49
Glasshouse St. W1—3B 34
Glasshouse Wlk. SE11—2H 59
Glasshouse Yd. EC1—2H 25
Glazbury Rd. W14—1A 52
Glebe Pl. SW3—4G 55
Gledhow Gdns. SW5—1B 54
Gledstanes Rd. W14—3A 52
Glendower Pl. SW7—6E 43
Glengall Ter. SE15—4H 63
Glentworth St. NW1—2B 20
Globe St. SE1—3B 50
Globe Yd. W1—1G 33
Gloucester Av. NW1—1F 9
Gloucester Ct. EC3—3F 39
Gloucester Gdns. W2—6B 18
Gloucester Ga. NW1—2F 9
  (in two parts)
Gloucester Ga. M. NW1—2F 9
Gloucester M. NW1—2F 9
Gloucester M. W. W2—6C 18
Gloucester Pl.—1B to 6C 20
  W1 1-127 & 10-118
  NW1 remainder
Gloucester Pl. M. W1—5C 20
Gloucester Rd. SW7—3B 42
Gloucester Sq. W2—1F 31

Gloucester St. SW1—3A 58
Gloucester Ter. W2—5H 17 to 2E 31
Gloucester Wlk. W8—1F 41
Gloucester Way. EC1—5D 12
Glynde M. SW3—5A 44
Glyn St. SE11—3H 59
Goat St. SE1—1G 51
Godfrey St. SW3—2H 55
Goding St. SE11—2H 59
Godliman St. EC4—1G 37
Godson St. N1—3C 12
Golborne Gdns. W10—2B 16
Golborne M. W10—4A 16
Golborne Rd. W10—4A 16
Golden La. EC1 & EC2—1H 25
Golden La. Est. EC1—2H 25
Golden Sq. W1—2B 34
Goldington Cres. NW1—2C 10
Goldington St. NW1—2D 10
Goldney Rd. W9—2E 17
Goldsmith St. EC2—6A 26
Goodge Pl. W1—4B 22
Goodge St. W1—4B 22
Goodman's Ct. E1—2H 39
Goodmans Yd. E1—2H 39
Goods Way. NW1—3E 11
Goodwin Ct. NW1—2C 10
Goodwins Ct. WC2—3F 35
Goodyear Pl. SE5—6B 62
Gophir La. EC4—2C 38
Gopsall St. N1—1C 14
Gordon Pl. W8—1F 41
Gordon Sq. WC1—1D 22
Gordon St. WC1—1C 22
Gorefield Pl. NW6—2E 5
Gore St. SW7—4C 42
Goring St. EC3—6F 27
Gorleston St. W14—6A 40
Gorsuch Pl. E2—4G 15
Gorsuch St. E2—4G 15
Gosfield St. W1—4H 21
Goslett Yd. WC2—6D 22
Goswell Pl. EC1—6F 13
Goswell Rd. EC1—4E 13 to 3H 25
Gough Sq. EC4—6D 24
Gough St. WC1—1B 24
Goulston St. E1—5H 27
Gower Ct. WC1—1C 22
Gower M. WC1—4D 22
Gower Pl. WC1—1C 22
Gower St. WC1—1C 22
Gracechurch Ct. EC3—2D 38
Gracechurch St. EC3—2D 38
Grafton M. W1—2A 22
Grafton Pl. NW1—5D 10
Grafton St. W1—3H 33
Grafton Way.—3A 22
  WC1 1-29 & 2-46
  W1 remainder
Graham St. N1—3G 13
Graham Ter. SW1—1D 56
Granary St. NW1—1C 10
Granby Bldgs. SE11—1A 60
Granby Ter. NW1—4A 10
Grand Av. EC1—4F 25
Grange Ct. WC2—1B 36
Grange Rd. SE1—4F 51
Grange, The. SE1—4G 51
Grange Wlk. SE1—4F 51
Grange Yd. SE1—4G 51
Grantbridge St. N1—2G 13
Grantham Pl. W1—6F 33
Grant St. N1—2C 12
Grantully Rd. W9—6G 5
Granville Pl. W1—1D 32
Granville Rd. NW6—3E & 3F 5
Granville Sq. WC1—5B 12
Granville St. WC1—5B 12
Grape St. WC2—6F 23
Gravel La. E1—6G 27
Gray's Inn Ct. WC1—4B 24
Gray's Inn Rd. WC1—4G 11 to 4C 24
Gray's Inn Sq. WC1—4B 24
Gray St. SE1—2E 49
  (in two parts)
Gray's Yd. W1—6E 21
Gt. Bell All. EC2—6C 26
Gt. Castle St. W1—6H 21

72

Gt. Central St. NW1—3A 20
Gt. Chapel St. W1—6C 22
Gt. College St. SW1—4F 47
Gt. Cumberland M. W1—1B 32
Gt. Cumberland Pl. W1—6B 20
Gt. Dover St. SE1—6B 50
Gt. Eastern St. EC2—6D 14
Gt. George St. SW1—2E 47
Gt. Guildford St. SE1—5H 37
Gt. James St. WC1—3A 24
Gt. Marlborough St. W1—1A 34
Gt. Maze Pond. SE1—6C 38 & 1C 50
Gt. Newport St. WC2—2E 35
Gt. New St. EC4—6D 24
Gt. Ormond St. WC1—3G 23
Gt. Percy St. WC1—5A to 4C 12
Gt. Peter St. SW1—4D 46 to 4F 47
Gt. Portland St. W1—2H 21
Gt. Pulteney St. W1—2B 34
Gt. Queen St. WC2—6G 23
Gt. Russell St. WC1—5D 22 to 4G 23
Gt. Saint Helens. EC3—6E 27
Gt. Saint Thomas Apostle. EC4—2A 38
Gt. Scotland Yd. SW1—5F 35
Gt. Smith St. SW1—3E 47
Gt. Suffolk St. SE1—5G 37 to 2H 49
Gt. Sutton St. EC1—2F 25
Gt. Swan All. EC2—5C 26
Gt. Titchfield St. W1—2H 21 to 6A 22
Gt. Tower St. EC3—2E 39
Gt. Trinity La. EC4—2A 38
Gt. Turnstile. WC1—5B 24
Gt. Western Rd.—2D 16
    W9 1-37 & 2-56
    W11 remainder
Gt. Winchester St. EC2—5D 26
Gt. Windmill St. W1—2C 34
Great Yd. SE1—1F 51
Greek Ct. W1—1E 35
Greek St. W1—6D 22
Green Arbour Ct. EC1—6F 25
Greenberry St. NW8—3G 7
Greencoat Pl. SW1—6B 46
Greencoat Row. SW1—5B 46
Green Dragon Ct. SE1—5C 38
Greenham Clo. SE1—3C 48
Greenhill's Rents. EC1—4F 25
Green's Ct. W1—2C 34
Green St. W1—2C 32
Green Wlk. SE1—4E 51
Greenwell St. W1—2H 21
Greenwood Ct. SW1—3B 58
Greet St. SE1—6D 36
Gregory Pl. W8—1G 41
Greig Ter. SE17—5G 61
Grendon St. NW8—1G 19
Grenville M. SW7—6C 42
Grenville Pl. SW7—5B 42
Grenville St. WC1—2G 23
Gresham St. EC2—6H 25
Gresse St. W1—5C 22
Greville M. NW6—1G 5
Greville Pl. NW6—2H 5
Greville Rd. NW6—2G 5 to 2A 6
Greville St. EC1—4C 24
Greycoat Pl. SW1—4C 46
Greycoat St. SW1—5C 46
Grey Eagle St. E1—3H 27
Greyfriars Pas. EC1—6G 25
Greyhound Ct. WC2—2B 36
Greyhound Rd. W6 & W14—4A 52
Greystoke Pl. EC4—5C 24
Grigg's Pl. SE1—4F 51
Grindal St. SE1—2C 48
Grittleton Rd. W9—1E 17
Grocer's Hall Ct. EC2—1B 38
Grocer's Hall Gdns. EC2—6B 26
Groom Pl. SW1—3F 45
Grosvenor Cotts. SW1—6D 44
Grosvenor Cres. SW1—2E 45
Grosvenor Cres. M. SW1—2D 44
Grosvenor Est. SW1—6D 46
Grosvenor Gdns. SW1—4G 45
Grosvenor Gdns. M. E. SW1—4G 45
Grosvenor Gdns. M. N. SW1—4G 45
Grosvenor Gdns. M. S. SW1—4G 45
Grosvenor Ga. W1—3C 32
Grosvenor Hill. W1—2G 33

Grosvenor Pk. SE5—6H 61
Grosvenor Pl. SW1—1E 45
Grosvenor Rd. SW1—4F 57 to 3E 59
Grosvenor Sq. W1—2E 33
Grosvenor St. W1—2F 33
Grosvenor Ter. SE5—6G 61
Grotto Ct. SE1—1G 49
Grotto Pas. W1—4E 21
Grove End Rd. NW8—4D 6
Grove Gdns. NW8—6H 7
Grove Hall Ct. NW8—4D 6
Groveland Ct. EC4—1A 38
Grove M. W11—6B 16
Guest St. EC1—2B 26
Guildhall Bldgs. EC2—6B 26
Guildhall Yd. EC2—6A & 6B 26
Guildhouse St. SW1—6A 46
Guilford Pl. WC1—2H 23
Guilford St. WC1—2G 23
Guinness Ct. NW8—1H 7
Guinness Sq. SE1—5E 51
Gunpowder Sq. EC4—6E 25
Gun St. E1—4G 27
Gunter Gro. SW10—6B 54
Gunterstone Rd. W14—1A 52
Guthrie St. SW3—2G 55
Gutter La. EC2—6H 25
Guy St. SE1—1D 50
Gwendwr Rd. W14—2A 52
Gwynne Pl. WC1—6B 12

Haberdasher Pl. N1—4D 14
Haberdasher St. N1—4C 14
Hackney Rd. E2—5G 15
Haggerston Rd. E8—1H 15
Halcomb St. N1—1E 15
Haldane Rd. SW6—6D 52
Half Moon Ct. EC1—4H 25
Half Moon Cres. N1—2B 12
Half Moon St. W1—5G 33
Halford Rd. SW6—6E 53
Halkin Arc. SW1—3C 44
Halkin M. SW1—3D 44
Halkin Pl. SW1—3D 44
Halkin St. SW1—2E 45
Hallam M. W1—3H 21
Hallam St. W1—2G to 4H 21
Hallfield Est. W2—6B 18
Hall Ga. NW8—5D 6
Hall Pl. W2—2D 18
Hall Rd. NW8—6C 6
Hall St. EC1—5F 13
Halpin Pl. SE17—1D 62
Halsey M. SW3—6A 44
Halsey St. SW3—6A 44
Hamilton Bldgs. EC2—1F 27
Hamilton Clo. NW8—6D 7
Hamilton Ct. W9—5B 6
Hamilton Gdns. NW8—4C 6
Hamilton M. W1—6F 33
Hamilton Pl. W1—6F 33
Hamilton Sq. SE1—1C 50
Hamilton Ter. NW8—3A 6
Hammersmith Rd. W14—6A 40
Hammett St. EC3—2H 39
Hamond Sq. N1—2E 15
Hampden Clo. NW1—3D 10
Hampden Gurney St. W1—1B 32
Hampstead Rd. NW1—2A 10
Hampton Clo. NW6—5F 5
Hampton St. SE17 & SE1—6G 49
Ham Yd. W1—2C 34
Hanbury M. N1—1A 14
Hanbury St. E1—3H 27
Hand Ct. WC1—4A 24
Handel St. WC1—1F 23
Hanging Sword All. EC4—1E 37
Hankey Pl. SE1—2C 50
Hanover Gdns. SE11—6C 60
Hanover Ga. NW1—5H 7
Hanover Pl. WC2—1G 35
Hanover Sq. W1—1H 33
Hanover St. W1—1H 33
Hanover Ter. NW1—6A 8
Hanover Ter. M. NW1—6A 8
Hanover Yd. N1—2G 13
Hans Cres. SW1—3B 44

Hanson St. W1—3A 22
Hans Pl. SW1—4B 44
Hans Rd. SW3—3A 44
Hans St. SW1—4B 44
Hanway Pl. W1—5D 22
Hanway St. W1—6D 22
Harbet Rd. W2—4F 19
Harcourt St. W1—4H 19
Harcourt Ter. SW10—3A 54
Harding Clo. SE17—5H 61
Hardwick St. EC1—5D 12
Hardwidge St. SE1—1E 51
Hare Ct. EC4—1C 36
Hare Wlk. N1—3F 15
Harewood Av. NW1—2H 19
Harewood Pl. W1—1H 33
Harewood Row. NW1—3A 20
Harleyford Rd. SE11—4H 59
Harleyford St. SE11—5C 60
Harley Gdns. SW10—3C 54
Harley Pl. W1—4F 21
Harley St. W1—2F 21
Harmsworth St. SE17—4E 61
Harold Est. SE1—5F 51
Harold Pl. SE11—3B 60
Harp All. EC4—6E 25
Harper Rd. SE1—3A 50
Harp La. EC3—3E 39
Harpur M. WC1—3H 23
Harpur St. WC1—3H 23
Harriet St. SW1—3C 44
Harriet Wlk. SW1—2C 44
Harrington Gdns. SW7—1A 54
Harrington Rd. SW7—6D 42
Harrington Sq. NW1—3A 10
Harrington St. NW1—4A 10
    (in two parts)
Harrison St. WC1—6G 11
Harrowby St. W1—5A 20
Harrow Pl. E1—5G 27
Harrow Rd.—1A 16 to 4F 19
    W2 1-281 & 2-322
    W9 283-421a & 324-570
    W10 remainder
Hartland Rd. NW6—2B 4
Hartshorn All. EC3—1F 39
Hart St. EC3—2F 39
Harvey's Bldgs. WC2—3G 35
Harvey St. N1—1D 14
Harvist Rd. NW6—3A 4
Hasker St. SW3—5A 44
Hassard St. E2—4H 15
Hastings Bldgs. SE1—4E 51
Hastings St. WC1—6F 11
Hatfields. SE1—5E 37
Hatherley Gro. W2—6H 17
Hatherley St. SW1—6B 46
Hatton Garden. EC1—3D 24
Hatton Pl. EC1—3D 24
Hatton Row. NW8—2E 19
Hatton St. NW8—2E 19
Hatton Wall. EC1—3D 24
Haunch of Venison Yd. W1—1G 33
Haverstock St. N1—4G 13
Hayden's Pl. W11—6B 16
Haydon St. EC3—1H 39
Haydon Wlk. E1—1H 39
Hayes Pl. NW1—3H 19
Hay Hill. W1—4H 33
Hayles St. SE11—5F 49
Haymarket. SW1—3D 34
Haymarket Arc. SW1—3C 34
Hayne St. EC1—3G 25
Hay's Galleria. SE1—5E 39
Hay's La. SE1—5D 38
Hay's M. W1—4F 33
Hayward's Pl. EC1—1E 25
Hazelmere Rd. NW6—1E 5
Hazel Way. SE1—5G 51
Hazlewood Cres. W10—2A 16
Headfort Pl. SW1—2E 45
Head's M. W11—1E 29
Hearn St. EC2—2F 27
Heathcote St. WC1—6H 11
Heather Wlk. W10—1A 16
Heddon St. W1—3A 34
Heiron St. SE17—5G 61
Heldar Ct. SE1—2D 50

Kean St. WC2—1H 35
Keats Pl. EC2—4C 26
Keeley St. WC2—6H 23
Kell St. SE1—3F 49
Kelso Pl. W8—4H 41
Kemble Ct. SE15—6F 63
Kemble St. WC2—1H 35
Kemp's Ct. W1—1C 34
Kempsford Gdns. SW5—3G 53
Kempsford Rd. SE11—1D 60
Kendall Pl. W1—5D 20
Kendal St. W2—1H 31
Kendrick M. SW7—6E 43
Kendrick Pl. SW7—6E 43
Kennet Rd. W9—1C 16
Kennet Wharf La. EC4—3A 38
Kennings Way. SE11—3E 61
Kennington Grn. SE11—4C 60
Kennington Gro. SE11—4A 60
Kennington La. SE11—4H 59 to 1F 61
Kennington Oval. SE11—5B 60
Kennington Pk. Gdns. SE11—5E 61
Kennington Pk. Pl. SE11—4E 61
Kennington Pk. Rd. SE11—6C 60
Kennington Rd.—3C 48 to 4D 60
  SE1 1-69 & 2-64
  SE11 remainder
Kenrick Pl. W1—4D 20
Kensal Rd. W10—1A 16
Kensington Chu. Ct. W8—2G 41
Kensington Chu. St. W8—4F 29
Kensington Chu. Wlk. W8—1G 41
Kensington Ct. W8—2A 42
Kensington Ct. M. W8—3A 42
Kensington Ct. Pl. W8—3A 42
Kensington Gdns. Sq. W2—1H 29
Kensington Ga. W8—3B 42
Kensington Gore. SW7—2D 42
Kensington Hall Gdns. W14—2C 52
Kensington High St.—5B 40 to 2H 41
  W8 1-353 & 2-280
  W14 remainder
Kensington Mall. W8—4F 29
Kensington Pal. Gdns. W8—4G 29
Kensington Pk. Gdns. W11—3C 28
Kensington Pk. M. W11—1B 28
Kensington Pk. Rd. W11—6B 16 to 4E 29
Kensington Pl. W8—5E 29
Kensington Rd. W8 & SW7—2A 42
Kensington Sq. W8—2H 41
Kentish Bldgs. SE1—6B 38
Kenton St. WC1—1F 23
Kent Pas. NW1—6A 8
Kent St. E2—2H 15
Kent Ter. NW1—6A 8
Kent Yd. SW7—2H 43
Kenway Rd. SW5—1G 53
Keppel Row. SE1—6H 37
Keppel St. WC1—3D 22
Keyse Rd. SE1—5H 51
Keystone Cres. N1—3H 11
Keyworth Pl. SE1—3G 49
Keyworth St. SE1—3F 49
Kiffen St. EC2—1D 26
Kilburn High Rd. NW6—1F 5
Kilburn La. W10 & W9—4A 4
Kilburn Pk. Rd. NW6—6E 5
Kilburn Pl. NW6—1G 5
Kilburn Priory. NW6—1G 5
Kildare Gdns. W2—6G 17
Kildare Ter. W2—6G 17
Killick St. N1—2H to 4H 11
Kilravock St. W10—5A 4
Kincardine Gdns. W9—2E 17
King Charles St. SW1—1E 47
King Edward St. EC1—6G 25
King Edward Wlk. SE1—4D 48
Kinghorn St. EC1—4G 25
King James St. SE1—3F 49
King John St. EC2—1F 27
Kinglake Est. SE17—2F 63
Kinglake St. SE17—3E 63
Kingly Ct. W1—2B 34
Kingly St. W1—1A 34
King & Queen St. SE17—1A 62
Kings Arms Yd. EC2—6B 26
King's Bench St. SE1—1F 49
King's Bench Wlk. EC4—2D 36

Kingscote St. EC4—2E 37
King's Cross Bri. WC1—4H 11
King's Cross Rd. WC1—4H 11
Kingsgate Pde. SW1—4B 46
King's Head Ct. EC3—3D 38
King's Head Yd. SE1—6C 38
Kingsland Rd.—5F 15
  E2 1-283 & 2-240
  E8 remainder
Kingsley M. W8—4A 42
King's M. WC1—3B 24
Kingsmill Ter. NW8—2E 7
King's Pl. SE1—3H 49
King Sq. EC1—6H 13
King's Rd.—6D 54 to 1C 56
  SW3 1-363 & 2-392
  SW10 remainder
King's Scholars' Pas. SW1—5A 46
King's Ter. NW1—1A 10
King St. EC2—1B 38
King St. SW1—5B 34
King St. WC2—2F 35
Kingsway. WC2—5H 23
Kingswood Av. NW6—1A 4
King William St. EC4—1C 38
Kinnerton Pl. N. SW1—2C 44
Kinnerton Pl. S. SW1—2C 44
Kinnerton St. SW1—2C 44
Kinnerton Yd. SW1—2C 44
Kinnoul Rd. W6—5A 52
Kinross St. SE1—2F 51
Kintore Way. SE1—5H 51
Kipling Est. SE1—2D 50
Kipling St. SE1—2C 50
Kirby Gro. SE1—1D 50
Kirby St. EC1—3D 24
Kirkman Pl. W1—4C 22
Kirk St. WC1—3A 24
Kirtling St. SW8—6B 58
Kirton Gdns. E2—5H 15
Kitson Rd. SE5—6B 62
Knaresborough Pl. SW5—6H 41
Knightrider Ct. EC4—2G 37
Knightrider St. EC4—1G 37
Knights Arc. SW1—2B 44
Knightsbridge.—2G 43 to 1D 44
  SW1 1-161 & 2-124
  SW7 remainder
Knightsbridge Ct. SW1—2B 44
Knightsbridge Grn. SW1—2B 44
Knights Wlk. SE11—1E 61
Knivett Rd. SW6—6E 53
Knox St. W1—3B 20
Kramer M. SW5—3G 53
Krupnik Pl. EC2—6F 15
Kynance M. SW7—4A 42
Kynance Pl. SW7—4B 42

Laburnum St. E2—1G 15
Lackington St. EC2—3C 26
Ladbroke Cres. W11—6A 16
Ladbroke Gdns. W11—2B 28
Ladbroke Gro.—5A 16 to 5C 28
  W11 1-137 & 2-108
  W10 remainder
Ladbroke M. W11—5B 28
Ladbroke Rd. W11—5B 28 to 4E 29
Ladbroke Sq. W11—4C 28
Ladbroke Ter. W11—4D 28
Ladbroke Wlk. W11—4D 28
Lafone St. SE1—1G 51
Lakeside Ter. EC4—4A 26
Lambert Jones M. EC2—4H 25
Lambeth Bri. SW1 & SE1—5G 47
Lambeth High St. SE1—6H 47
Lambeth Hill. EC4—2H 37
Lambeth Pal Rd. SE1—5H 47
Lambeth Rd. SE1—5H 47 to 3E 49
Lambeth Wlk. SE11—1A 60 to 5C 48
Lamb's Bldgs. EC1—2B 26
Lamb's Conduit Pas. WC1—4A 24
Lamb's Conduit St. WC1—2H 23 & 3A 24
Lamb's M. N1—1F 13
Lamb's Pas. EC1—3B 26
Lamb St. E1—3G 27
Lambton Pl. W11—2D 28
Lamb Wlk. SE1—2E 51

Lamlash St. SE11—5F 49
Lamont Rd. SW10—6D 54
Lamont Rd. Pas. SW10—5D 54
Lanark Pl. W9—1D 18
Lanark Rd. W9—3H 5
Lancashire Ct. W1—2G 33
Lancaster Ga. W2—2C & 3C 30
Lancaster M. W2—2D 30
Lancaster Pl. WC2—2H 35
Lancaster Rd. W11—6A 16
Lancaster St. SE1—2F 49
Lancaster Ter. W2—2E 31
Lancaster Wlk. W2 & SW7
                    —3D 30 to 1D 42
Lancefield St. W10—4B & 5B 4
Lancelot Pl. SW7—2A 44
Lancing St. NW1—5D 10
Landon Pl. SW1—3B 44
Lane, The. NW8—3B 6
Lanfrey Pl. W14—3C 52
Langdale Clo. SE17—4H 61
Langford Clo. NW8—2C 6
Langford Pl. NW8—3C 6
Langham Pl. W1—5H 21
Langham St. W1—4H 21
Langley Ct. WC2—2G 35
Langley La. SW8—5H 59
Langley St. WC2—1F 35
Langthorn Ct. EC2—5C 26
Langton Clo. WC1—6B 12
Langton St. SW10—6C 54
Langtry Rd. NW8—1H 5
Lanhill Rd. W9—1E 17
Lansdowne Cres. W11—3B 28
Lansdowne M. W11—5B 28
Lansdowne Pl. SE1—4D 50
Lansdowne Rise. W11—3A 28
Lansdowne Rd. W11—2A to 5C 28
Lansdowne Row. W1—4H 33
Lansdowne Ter. WC1—2H 23
Lansdowne Wlk. W11—4B 28
Lant St. SE1—1H 49
Lapford Clo. W9—6C 4
Larcom St. SE17—1D 62
Latham Ct. SW5—1E 53
Lauderdale Mans. W9—6H 5
Lauderdale Rd. W9—6H 5
Lauderdale Tower. EC2—4H 25
Laud St. SE11—3H 59
Launcelot St. SE1—2C 48
Launceston Pl. W8—4B 42
Laundry Rd. W6—6A 52
Laurence Pountney Hill. EC4—2C 38
Laurence Pountney La. EC4—3C 38
Lavender Clo. SW3—5F 55
Laverton M. SW5—1H 53
Laverton Pl. SW5—1H 53
Lavina Gro. N1—2H 11
Lavington St. SE1—5G 37
Lawn La. SW8—5H 59
Lawrence La. EC2—6A 26
Lawrence St. SW3—5G 55
Law St. SE1—4D 50
Laxton Pl. NW1—1H 21
Laystall St. EC1—2C 24
Layton Rd. N1—2D 12
Layton's Bldgs. SE1—1B 50
Lazenby Ct. WC2—2F 35
Leadenhall Mkt. EC3—1D 38
Leadenhall Pl. EC3—1E 39
Leadenhall St. EC3—1E 39
Leake Ct. SE1—2B 48
Leake St. SE1—1B 48
Leamington Rd. Vs. W11—5D 16
Leather La. EC1—3C 24
Leathermarket St. SE1—2D 50
Lecky St. SW7—2E 55
Ledbury M. N. W11—2E 29
Ledbury M. W. W11—2E 29
Ledbury Rd. W11—6D 16
Lee Ho. EC2—4A 26
Leeke St. WC1—4H 11
Lees Pl. W1—2D 32
Leicester Ct. WC2—2E 35
Leicester Pl. WC2—2E 35
Leicester Sq. WC2—3D 34
Leicester St. WC2—3D 34

Leigh Hunt St. SE1—1H 49
(in two parts)
Leigh Pl. EC1—4C 24
Leigh St. WC1—6F 11
Leinster Gdns. W2—1B 30
Leinster M. W2—3B 30
Leinster Pl. W2—1B 30
Leinster Rd. NW6—4E 5
Leinster Sq. W2—1G 29
Leinster Ter. W2—2B 30
Leith Mans. W9—6G 5
Lennox Gdns. SW1—5A 44
Lennox Gdns. M. SW1—5A 44 .
Lenthall Pl. SW7—6C 42
Leonard St. EC2—1C 26
Leopards Ct. EC1—3C 24
Leo Yd. EC1—2F 25
Leroy St. SE1—5E 51
Leverett St. SW3—6A 44
Leverington St. N1—5D 14
Lever St. EC1—6G 13
Lewen's Ct. EC1—6H 13
Lewisham St. SW1—2D 46
Lexham Gdns. W8—5F to 6H 41
Lexham Gdns. M. W8—5H 41
Lexham M. W8—5F 41
Lexham Wlk. W8—5H 41
Lexington St. W1—1B 34
Leyden St. E1—5G 27
Library St. SE1—3F 49
Lidlington Pl. NW1—3B 10
Light Horse Ct. SW3—3D 56
Ligonier St. E2—6G 15
Lilac Pl. SE11—1A 60
Lilestone St. NW8—1G 19
Lillie Rd. SW6—6A 52 to 4F 53
Lillie Yd. SW6—4F 53
Lillington Gdns. Est. SW1—1C 58
Lily Pl. EC1—3E 25
Limerston St. SW10—6B 54
Lime St. EC3—2E 39
Lime St. Pas. EC3—1E 39
Lincoln's Inn Fields. WC2—6A 24
Lincoln St. SW3—1B 56
Linden Gdns. W2—3F 29
Linden M. W2—4F 29
Lindsay Sq. SW1—3D 58
Lindsey St. EC1—4G 25
Linhope St. NW1—1A 20
Lintaine Clo. W6—6A 52
Linton St. N1—1A 14
Lisgar Ter. W14—6B 40
Lisle St. WC2—2D 34
Lisson Gro.—6E 7 to 3A 20
NW1 1-135 & 2-116
NW8 remainder
Lisson St. NW1—3G 19
Litchfield St. WC2—2E 35
Lit. Albany St. NW1—6H 9
Lit. Argyll St. W1—1A 34
Lit. Boltons, The. SW10—3A 54
Lit. Britain. EC1—4G to 5H 25
Lit. Chester St. SW1—3F 45
Lit. College La. EC4—2B 38
Lit. College St. SW1—4F 47
Lit. Dean's Yd. SW1—3F 47
Lit. Dorrit Ct. SE1—1A 50
Lit. Edward St. NW1—4G 9
Lit. Essex St. WC2—2A 38
Lit. George St. SW1—2E 47
Lit. Marlborough St. W1—1A 34
Lit. Newport St. WC2—2E 35
Lit. New St. EC4—6D 24
Lit. Portland St. W1—5H 21
Lit. Russell St. WC1—5F 23
Lit. Saint James's St. SW1—6A 34
Lit. Sanctuary. SW1—2E 47
Lit. Smith St. SW1—4E 47
Lit. Somerset St. E1—1H 39
Lit. Titchfield St. W1—5A 22
Lit. Trinity La. EC4—2A 38
(in two parts)
Liverpool Gro. SE17—3A 62
Liverpool Rd. N1—1D 12
Liverpool St. EC2—5E 27
Livonia St. W1—1C 34
Lizard St. EC1—6A 14
Lloyd Baker St. WC1—6B & 5C 12

Lloyd's Av. EC3—1F 39
Lloyd Sq. WC1—5C 12
Lloyd's Row. EC1—5E 13
Lloyd St. WC1—5C 12
Locksfield. SE17—1C 62
Lockyer Est. SE1—1D 50
Lockyer St. SE1—2C 50
Lodge Rd. NW8—6F 7
Logan M. W8—6E 41
Logan Pl. W8—6E 41
Lolesworth Clo. E1—4H 27
Lollard St. SE11—6B 48
(in two parts)
Loman St. SE1—1G 49
Lombard Ct. EC3—2D 38
Lombard La. EC4—1D 36
Lombard St. EC3—1C 38
Lombardy Pl. W2—3H 29
Loncroft Rd. SE5—4F 63
London Bri. SE1 & EC4—4C 38
London Bri. St. SE1—5C 38
London Bri. Wlk. SE1—5D 38
London M. W2—6E 19
London Pavillion. W1—3C 34
London Rd. SE1—3F 49
London St. EC3—2F 39
London St. W2—6E 19
London Wall. EC2—5A to 5D 26
Long Acre. WC2—2F 35
Longfield Est. SE1—6H 51
Longford St. NW1—1H 21
Longhope Clo. SE15—6G 63
Longlands Ct. W11—2D 28
Long La. EC1—4G 25
Long La. SE1—1B 50
Longmoore St. SW1—1A 58
Longridge Rd. SW5—1E 53
Long's Ct. WC2—3E 35
Longshott Cl. SW5—1F 53
Long St. E2—5G 15
Longville Rd. SE11—6F 49
Long Wlk. SE1—3F 51
Long Yd. WC1—2H 23
Lonsdale M. W11—1D 28
Lonsdale Rd. NW6—2B 4
Lonsdale Rd. W11—1C 28
Lonsdale Yd. W11—3E 29
Lord Hills Bri. W2—5H 17
Lord Hills Rd. W2—3H 17
Lord North St. SW1—4F 47
Lordship Pl. SW3—5G 55
Lords View. NW8—5F 7
Lorenzo St. WC1—4A 12
Lorne Clo. NW8—6H 7
Lorrimore Rd. SE17—5G 61
Lorrimore Sq. SE17—4G 61
Lothbury. EC2—6C 26
Lothrop St. W10—5A 4
Loudoun Rd. NW8—1C to 3D 6
Loughborough St. SE11—3B 60
Lovat La. EC3—3D 38
Love La. EC2—5A 26
Lover's Wlk. W1—4D 32
Lwr. Belgrave St. SW1—4F 45
Lwr. Grosvenor Pl. SW1—3G 45
Lwr. James St. W1—2B 34
Lwr. John St. W1—3B 34
Lwr. Marsh. SE1—2B 48
Lwr. Robert St. WC2—4G 35
Lwr. Sloane St. SW1—1C 56
Lwr. Thames St. EC3—3D 38
Lowndes Clo. SW1—4E 45
Lowndes Ct. SW1—3C 44
Lowndes Ct. W1—1A 34
Lowndes Pl. SW1—4D 44
Lowndes Sq. SW1—2C 44
Lowndes St. SW1—3C 44
Lowther Gdns. SW7—3E 43
Loxham St. WC1—5G 11
Lucan Pl. SW3—6G 43
Ludgate Cir. EC4—1E 37
Ludgate Ct. EC4—1F 37
Ludgate Hill. EC4—1F 37
Ludgate Sq. EC4—1F 37
Ludlow St. EC1—1G 25
Luke St. EC2—1D 26

Lumley Ct. WC2—3G 35
Lumley St. W1—1E 33
Lupus St. SW1—4H 57 to 2D 58
Luscombe Way. SW8—6F 59
Luton St. NW8—2F 19
Luxborough St. W1—3D 20
Lyall M. SW1—4D 44
Lyall M. W. SW1—5D 44
Lyall St. SW1—4D 44
Lydford Rd. W9—6D 4
Lydney Clo. SE15—6F 63
Lygon Pl. SW1—4G 45
Lynton Rd. NW6—1C 4
Lynton Rd. SE1—1H 63
Lyons Pl. NW8—2E 19
Lyons Wlk. W14—6A 40
Lytham St. SE17—3B 62

Mabledon Pl. WC1—5E 11
McAuley Clo. SE1—4C 48
Macclesfield Rd. EC1—4H 13
Macclesfield St. W1—2D 34
McCoid Way. SE1—2H 49
Macfarren Pl. NW1—2E 21
McGregor Rd. W11—5C 16
Mackennal St. NW8—3H 7
Macklin St. WC2—6G 23
Mackworth St. NW1—4A 10
McLeod's M. SW7—5A 42
Macleod St. SE17—4A 62
Maclise Rd. W14—4A 40
Macroom Rd. W9—5D 4
Maddock Way. SE17—5F 61
Maddox St. W1—2H 33
Madron St. SE17—2F 63
Magdalen St. SE1—6E 39
Magee St. SE11—5C 60
Magpie All. EC1   1D 36
Maida Av. W2—3C 18
Maida Vale. W9—3H 5 to 1D 18
Maiden La. WC2—3G 35
Maidstone Bldgs. SE1—6B 38
Mail Coach Yd. E2—4F 15
Makins St. SW3—1H 55
Malet Pl. WC1—2D 22
Malet St. WC1—2D 22
Mallord St. SW3—4E 55
Mallory St. NW8—1H 19
Mallow St. EC1—1C 26
Mall, The. SW1—5E 35
Malta St. EC1—6F 13
Maltby St. SE1—2G 51
Malton M. W10—5A 16
Maltravers St. WC2—2B 36
Malvern Clo. W10—4B 16
Malvern Gdns. NW6—4D 4
Malvern M. NW6—5E 5
Malvern Pl. W9—4D 4
Malvern Rd. NW6—4D 4
Manchester Dri. W10—2A 16
Manchester M. W1—5D 20
Manchester Sq. W1—5E 21
Manchester St. W1—4D 20
Manciple St. SE1—2C 50
Mandela St. NW1—1B 10
Mandela Way. SE1—6E 51
Mandeville Pl. W1—6E 21
Manette St. W1—1D 34
Manningford Clo. EC1—5F 13
Manor M. NW6—1G 5
Manor Pl. SE17—3G 61
Manresa Rd. SW3—3F 55
Mansell St. E1—1H 39
Mansfield M. W1—4G 21
Mansfield St. W1—4G 21
Mansion Ho. Pl. EC4—1C 38
Mansion Ho. St. EC2—1C 38
Manson M. SW7—6D 42
Manson Pl. SW7—1D 54
Maple M. NW6—2G 5
Maple Pl. W1—3B 22
Maple St. W1—3A 22
Marban Rd. W9—4C 4
Marble Arch. W2 & W1—2B 32
Marchbank Rd. W14—4D 52
Marchmont St. WC1—1F 23
Marcia Rd. SE1—1F 63

Margaret Ct. W1—6A 22
Margaret St. W1—6H 21 to 5B 22
Margaretta Ter. SW3—4H 55
Margery St. WC1—6C 12
Marigold All. SE1—4E 37
Market Ct. W1—6A 22
Market M. W1—5F 33
Market Pl. W1—6A 22
Market, The. WC2—2G 35
Markham Pl. SW3—2A 56
Markham Sq. SW3—2A 56
Markham St. SW3—2A 56
Mark La. EC3—2F 39
Mark St. EC2—1D 26
Marlborough Bldgs. SW3—6H 43
Marlborough Clo. SE17—1G 61
Marlborough Ct. W1—1A 34
Marlborough Ga. Stables. W2—2D 30
Marlborough Hill. NW8—1D 6
Marlborough Pl. NW8—3B 6
Marlborough Rd. SW1—6B 34
Marlborough St. SW3—1G 55
Marloes Rd. W8—4G 41
Marne St. W10—5A 4
Marshall Ho. SE1—4F 51
Marshall St. W1—1B 34
Marshalsea Rd. SE1—1A 50
Marsham Ct. SW1—6E 47
Marsham St. SW1—4E 47
Marsland Clo. SE17—3G 61
Martin La. EC4—2C 38
Martlett Ct. WC2—1G 35
Mart St. WC2—2G 35
Mary Flux Ct. SW5—2H 53
Marylands Rd. W9—2F 17
Marylebone Fly-over. W2 & NW1—4F 19
Marylebone High St. W1—3E & 4E 21
Marylebone La. W1—5E 21
Marylebone M. W1—5F 21
Marylebone Pas. W1—5B 22
Marylebone Rd. NW1—3A 20 to 2H 21
Marylebone St. W1—4E 21
Marylee Way. SE11—1B 60
Mary St. N1—1A 14
Mary Ter. NW1—1H 9
Mason's Arms M. W1—1H 33
Mason's Av. EC2—6B 26
Mason's Pl. EC1—5G 13
Mason's St. SE17—6D 50
Mason's Yd. SW1—4B 34
Massinger St. SE17—6E 51
Matheson Rd. W14—1C 52
Mathews Yd. WC2—6F 23
Matthew Parker St. SW1—2E 47
Maunsel St. SW1—6D 46
Mayfair Pl. W1—5H 33
Maygood St. N1—2B 12
Mays Ct. WC2—3F 35
May St. W14—3C 52
Meadcroft Rd. SE11—5E 61
(in two parts)
Meadow M. SW8—6A 60
Meadow Rd. SW8—6A 60
Meadow Row. SE11—5H 49
Mead Row. SE1—4C 48
Meakin Est. SE1—4E 51
Meard St. W1—1C 34
Mecklenburgh Pl. WC1—1H 23
Mecklenburgh Sq. WC1—1H 23
Mecklenburgh St. WC1—6H 11
Medburn St. NW1—2C 10
Medway St. SW1—5D 46
Melbourne Pl. WC2—1A 36
Melbury Ct. W8—4D 40
Melbury Rd. W14—4C 40
Melbury Ter. NW1—2A 20
Melcombe Pl. NW1—3A 20
Melcombe St. NW1—2B 20
Melina Pl. NW8—5D 6
Melior Pl. SE1—1E 51
Melior St. SE1—1D 50
Melon Pl. W8—6G 29
Melton Ct. SW7—6E 43
Melton St. NW1—6C 10
Memel Ct. EC1—2H 25
Memel St. EC1—2H 25
Mendora Rd. SW6—6B 52
Mepham St. SE1—6B 36

Mercer St. WC2—1E 35
Meredith St. EC1—6E 13
Merlin St. WC1—6C 12
Mermaid Ct. SE1—1B 50
Merrick Sq. SE1—3B 50
Merrington Rd. SW6—5F 53
Merritt's Bldgs. EC2—2D 26
Merrow St. SE17—4B 62
Merrow Wlk. SE17—2D 62
Methley St. SE11—3D 60
Meymott St. SE1—5E 37
Micawber St. N1—4A 14
Micklethwaite Rd. SW6—6F 53
Middlesex Pas. EC1—4G 25
Middlesex St. E1—4F 27
Middle St. EC1—4G 25
Middle Temple La. EC4—1C 36
Middleton Bldgs. W1—4A 22
Middle Yd. SE1—5D 38
Midford Pl. W1—2B 22
Midhope St. WC1—5G 11
Midland Rd. NW1—3E 11
Milborne Gro. SW10—4C 54
Milcote St. SE1—2F 49
Miles Pl. NW8—4F 19
Miles St. SW8—5F 59
Milford La. WC2—1B 36
Milk St. EC2—6A 26
Millbank. SW1—4F 47 to 2E 59
Miller St. NW1—2A 10
Millman M. WC1—2H 23
Millman St. WC1—2A 24
Mill Row. N1—1F 15
Mills Ct. EC2—6E 15
Millstream Rd. SE1—3H 51
Mill St. W1—2H 33
Milman's St. SW10—6E 55
Milner St. SW3—6A 44
Milroy Wlk. SE1—4E 37
Milton Ct. EC2—3B 26
Milton St. EC2—3B 26
Milverton St. SE11—3D 60
Mina Rd. SE17—3F 63
Mincing La. EC3—2E 39
Minera M. SW1—6E 45
Miniver Pl. EC4—2A 38
Miniver St. SE1—2F 49
Minnow Wlk. SE17—1F 63
Minories. EC3—1G 39
Mintern St. N1—2C 14
Mint St. SE1—1H 49
Missenden. SE17—3D 62
Mitchell St. EC1—1H 25
Mitre Ct. EC2—6A 26
Mitre Ct. EC4—1D 36
Mitre Rd. SE1—1D 48
Mitre Sq. EC3—1G 39
Mitre St. EC3—1F 39
Model Bldgs. WC1—6B 12
Modern Ct. EC4—6E 25
Molyneux St. W1—5H 19
Monck St. SW1—4E 47
Moncorvo Clo. SW7—3G 43
Monkton St. SE11—6D 48
Monkwell Sq. EC2—4A 26
Monmouth Pl. W2—1G 29
Monmouth Rd. W2—1G 29
Monmouth St. WC2—1F 35
Montague Clo. SE1—5C 38
Montague Pl. WC1—4E 23
Montague St. WC1—3F 23
Montagu Mans. W1—4C 20
Montagu M. N. W1—4B 20
Montagu M. S. W1—6B 20
Montagu M. W. W1—5B 20
Montagu Pl. W1—5B 20
Montagu Row. W1—4C 20
Montagu Sq. W1—5B 20
Montagu St. W1—6C 20
Montclare St. E2—6H 15
Monteagle Ct. N1—3F 15
Montford Pl. SE11—4C 60
Montpelier M. SW7—3H 43
Montpelier Pl. SW7—3H 43
Montpelier Sq. SW7—2H 43
Montpelier St. SW7—3H 43
Montpelier Ter. SW7—2H 43
Montpelier Wlk. SW7—3H 43

Montreal Pl. WC2—2A 36
Montrose Av. NW6—2A 4
Montrose Ct. SW7—2F 43
Montrose Pl. SW1—2E 45
Monument St. EC3—3D 38
Moore St. SW3—6B 44
Moorfields. EC2—4C 26
Moorfields Highwalk. EC2—5B 26
(in two parts)
Moorgate. EC2—6C 26
Moorgate Pl. EC2—5C 26
Moorhouse Rd. W2—6E 17
Moor La. EC2—4B 26
Moor Pl. EC2—4C 26
Moor St. W1—1E 35
Mora St. EC1—5A 14
Moravian Pl. SW10—6E 55
Morecambe St. SE17—1B 62
Moreland St. EC1—5G 13
Moreton Pl. SW1—2B 58
Moreton St. SW1—2C 58
Moreton Ter. SW1—2B 58
Moreton Ter. M. N. SW1—2B 58
Moreton Ter. M. S. SW1—3B 58
Morgan Rd. W10—4C 16
Morgan's La. SE1—5E 39
Morley St. SE1—3D 48
Mornington Av. W14—1C 52
Mornington Cres. NW1—2A 10
Mornington Pl. NW1—3H 9
Mornington St. NW1—2H 9
Mornington Ter. NW1—1G 9
Morocco St. SE1—2E 51
Morpeth Ter. SW1—5A 46
Morshead Mans. W9—6G 5
Morshead Rd. W9—5G 5
Mortimer Cres. NW6—1H 5
Mortimer Est. NW6—1H 5
Mortimer Mkt. WC1—2C 22
Mortimer Pl. NW6—1H 5
Mortimer St. W1—5H 21
Morton M. SW5—6H 41
Morton Pl. SE1—4C 48
Morwell St. WC1—5D 22
Moscow Pl. W2—2H 29
Moscow Rd. W2—2G 29
Mossop St. SW3—6H 43
Motcomb St. SW1—3C 44
Motley Av. EC2—1E 27
Mountjoy Ho. EC2—4A 26
Mt. Mills. EC1—6G 13
Mt. Pleasant. WC1—2B 24
Mount Row. W1—3F 33
Mount St. W1—4D 32
Moxon St. W1—4E 21
Moylan Rd. W6—6A 52
Mozart St. W10—6B 4
Mulberry Wlk. SW3—4E 55
Mulgrave Rd. SW6—5C 52
Mulready St. NW8—2G 19
Mulvaney Way. SE1—2D 50
Mumford Ct. EC2—6A 26
Mund St. W14—3C 52
Mundy St. N1—5E 15
Munro M. W10—3A 16
Munro Ter. SW10—6E 55
Munster Sq. NW1—6H 9
Munton Rd. SE17—6B 50
Muriel St. N1—2B & 1B 12
Murphy St. SE1—2C 48
Murray Gro. N1—4B 14
Musard Rd. W6—5A 52
Muscovy St. EC3—3F 39
Museum St. WC1—5F 23
Myddelton Pas. EC1—5D 12
Myddelton Sq. EC1—4D 12
Myddelton St. EC1—6D 12
Myddelton Ho. WC1—4B 12
Mylne St. EC1—4C 12

Nags Head Ct. EC1—2A 26
Nailsworth St. SE15—6E 63
Nantes Pas. E1—3G 27
Napier Clo. W14—4B 40
Napier Gro. N1—3B 14
Napier Pl. W14—4B 40
Napier Rd. W14—4B 40

Nash St. NW1—5G 9
Nassau St. W1—4A 22
Nathaniel Clo. E1—4H 27
Navarre St. E2—6G 15
Nazrul St. E2—4G 15
Neal St. WC2—6F 23
Neal's Yd. WC2—1F 35
Neate St. SE5—5E 63
Neathouse Pl. SW1—5A 46
Neckinger. SE1—3H 51
Needham Rd. W11—1E 29
Nelson Clo. NW6—1D 4
Nelson Pas. EC1—5A 14
Nelson Pl. N1—4F 13
Nelson Sq. SE1—6F 37
Nelson Ter. N1—4F 13
Netherton Gro. SW10—5C 54
Netley St. NW1—6A 10
Nettleton Ct. EC2—5H 25
Nevern Pl. SW5—1F 53
Nevern Rd. SW5—1E 53
Nevern Sq. SW5—1F 53
Neville Clo. NW1—3E 11
Neville Clo. NW6—3D 4
Neville Rd. NW6—3D 4
Neville St. SW7—2E 55
Neville Ter. SW7—2E 55
New Bond St. W1—1G 33
New Bri. St. EC4—1E 37
New Broad St. EC2—5D 26
Newburgh St. W1—1B 34
New Burlington M. W1—2A 34
New Burlington Pl. W1—2A 34
New Burlington St. W1—2A 34
Newburn St. SE11—3B 60
Newbury St. EC1—4H 25
Newcastle Clo. EC4—5E 25
Newcastle Ct. EC4—2B 38
Newcastle Pl. W2—1F 19
Newcastle Row. EC1—2E 25
New Cavendish St. W1—5E 21 to 3A 22
New Change. EC4—1H 37
New Church Rd. SE5—6C 62
Newcombe St. W8—4F 29
Newcomen St. SE1—6B 38
New Compton St. WC2—1E 35
New Ct. EC4—1C 36
Newcourt St. NW8—3G 7
New Coventry St. W1—3D 34
Newent Clo. SE15—6E 63
New Era Est. N1—1E 15
New Fetter La. EC4—6D 24
Newgate St. EC1—6F 25
New Goulston St. E1—5G 27
Newham's Row. SE1—3F 51
Newington Butts.—1F 61
 SE1 2-22
 SE11 remainder
Newington Causeway. SE1—4G 49
Newington Ind. Est. SE17—1G 61
New Inn B'way. EC2—1F 27
New Inn Pas. WC2—1A 36
New Inn Sq. EC2—1F 27
New Inn St. EC2—1F 27
New Inn Yd. EC2—1F 27
New Kent Rd. SE1—5H 49
New London St. EC3—2F 39
Newman Pas. W1—5C 22
Newman's Ct. EC3—1D 38
Newman's Row. WC2—5B 24
Newman St. W1—5B 22
Newman Yd. W1—5C 22
Newnham Ter. SE1—3C 48
New North Pl. EC2—1E 27
New North Rd. N1—1B to 4D 14
New North St. WC1—3H 23
New Oxford St. WC1—6E to 5G 23
Newport Ct. WC2—2E 35
Newport Pl. WC2—2E 35
Newport St. SE11—1A 60
New Quebec St. W1—6C 20
New Ride. SW7 & SW1—1F 43 to 1C 55
New Row. WC2—2F 35
New Spring Gdns. Wlk. SE11—3G 59
New Sq. WC2—6B 24
New St. EC2—5F 27
New St. Hill. EC4—6D 24

New St. Sq. EC4—6D 24
Newton Rd. W2—6G 17
Newton St. WC2—5G 23
New Turnstile. WC1—5H 23
New Union St. EC2—4B 26
New Wharf Rd. N1—2H 11
Nicholas La. EC4—2C 38
Nicholas Pas. EC4—2C 38
Nicholson St. SE1—5F 37
Nichol's Sq. E2—3H 15
 (in two parts)
Nile St. N1—5B 14
Nile Ter. SE15—3H 63
Nine Elms La. SW8—6B 58
Noble St. EC2—5H 25
Noel Rd. N1—2F 13
Noel St. W1—6B 22
Norfolk Cres. W2—6H 19
Norfolk Pl. W2—6F 19
Norfolk Rd. NW8—1F 7
Norfolk Row. SE11—5A 48
Norfolk Sq. W2—6E 19
Norfolk Sq. M. W2—1F 31
Norland Pl. W11—6A 28
Norland Sq. W11—5A 28
Normand Gdns. W14—4B 52
Normand M. W14—4B 52
Normand Rd. W14—4B 52
Norman's Bldgs. EC1—6H 13
Norman St. EC1—6H 13
Norris St. SW1—4D 34
Northampton Rd. EC1—1D 24
Northampton Row. EC1—6D 12
Northampton Sq. EC1—5F 13
N. Audley St. W1—1D 32
N. Bank. NW8—5G 7
Northburgh St. EC1—1G 25
N. Carriage Dri. W2—3F 31
N. Carriage Way. N2—2H 31
North Carriage Way. N2—2H 31
Northchurch. SE17—2C 62
 (in three parts)
North Ct. W1—3B 22
North Cres. WC1—3C 22
Northdown St. N1—3H 11
Northeast Ter. N1—3D 12
N. End Cres. W14—1B 52
N. End Rd.—6A 40 to 6E 53
 W14 1-313 & 2-236
 SW6 remainder
N. Flower Wlk. W2—3C 30
N. Gower St. NW1—6B 10
Northington St. WC1—3A 24
Northleach Ct. SE15—6E 63
North M. WC1—2B 24
Northport St. N1—1D 14
N. Ride. W2—3F 31
North Row. W1—2C 32
North Ter. SW3—5G 43
Northumberland All. EC3—1G 39
Northumberland Av. WC2—4F 35
Northumberland Pl. W2—6F 17
Northumberland St. WC2—4F 35
North Wlk. W2—4H 29 to 3E 31
Northwest Pl. N1—2D 12
N. Wharf Rd. W2—5D 18
Northwick Clo. NW8—1E 19
Northwick Ter. NW8—1D 18
Norton Folgate. E1—3F 27
Norwich St. EC4—5D 24
Nottingham Ct. WC2—1F 35
Nottingham Pl. W1—3D 20
Nottingham St. W1—3D 20
Nottingham Ter. NW1—2D 20
Notting Hill Ga. W11—4E 29
Nugent Ter. NW8—4C 6
Nun Ct. EC2—5C 26
Nutbourne St. W10—5A 4
Nutford Pl. W1—6A 20
Nuttall St. N1—2F 15

Oakden St. SE11—6D 48
Oakey La. SE1—3C 22
Oakfield St. SW10—4B 54
Oakington Rd. W9—1F 17
Oakley Cres. EC1—4G 13
Oakley Gdns. SW3—4H 55
Oakley Pl. SE1—3H 63

Oakley Sq. NW1—3B 10
Oakley St. SW3—4G 55
Oak Tree Rd. NW8—5F 7
Oakwood Ct. W14—3B 40
Oakwood La. W14—3B 40
Oat La. EC2—5A 26
Observatory Gdns. W8—1F 41
Occupation Rd. SE17—2H 61
Octagon Arc. EC2—4E 27
Odhams Wlk. WC2—1G 35
Offley Rd. SW9—6C 60
Ogle St. W1—4A 22
Old Bailey. EC4—6F 25
Old Barge Ho. All. SE1—4D 36
Old Barrack Yd. SW1—1D 44
Old Bond St. W1—4A 34
Old Brewer's Yd. WC2—1F 35
Old Broad St. EC2—6D 26
Old Brompton Rd.—4F 53 to 6F 43
 SW7 1-133 & 2-146
 SW5 remainder
Old Bldgs. WC2—6C 24
Old Burlington St. W1—2A 34
Oldbury Pl. W1—3E 21
Old Castle St. E1—5H 27
Old Cavendish St. W1—6G 21
Old Change Ct. EC4—1H 37
Old Chelsea M. SW3—6F 55
Old Church St. SW3—3E to 6G 55
Old Compton St. W1—2D 34
Old Ct. Pl. W8—1H 41
Old Fish St. Hill. EC4—2H 37
Old Gloucester St. WC1—3G 23
Old Jewry. EC2—1B 38
Old Kent Rd. SE1—6E 51
Old Manor Yd. SW5—2G 53
Old Marylebone Rd. NW1—5H 19
Old Nichol St. E2—1G 27
Old North Ct. WC1   III D0
Old Palace Yd. SW1—3F 47
Old Paradise St. SE11—6A 48
Old Pk. La. W1—6F 33
Old Pye St. SW1—4D 46
Old Quebec St. W1—1C 32
Old Queen St. SW1—2D 46
Old Seacoal La. EC4—6F 25
Old Sq. WC2—5B 24
Old St. EC1—2H 25 to 5F 15
Olivers Yd. EC1—1C 26
Olney Rd. SE17—5G 61
Olympia M. W2—3A 30
Olympia Way. W14—4A 40
O'Meara St. SE1—6A 38
Omega Pl. N1—4H 11
Ongar Rd. SW6—4E 53
Onslow Gdns. SW7—2D 54
Onslow M. E. SW7—1E 55
Onslow M. W. SW7—1E 55
Onslow Sq. SW7—6F 43 to 1E 55
Onslow St. EC1—3D 24
Ontario St. SE1—4G 49
Opal St. SE11—1E 61
Orange St. WC2—4D 34
Orange Yd. W1—6D 22
Oratory La. SW3—2F 55
Orb St. SE17—1C 62
Orchard Clo. W10—4B 16
Orchardson St. NW8—2E 19
Orchard Sq. W14—4B 52
Orchard St. W1—1D 32
Orde Hall St. WC1—3H 23
Ordnance Hill. NW8—1E 7
Ordnance M. NW8—2F 7
Orient St. SE11—5E 49
Orme Ct. W2—3H 29
Orme Ct. M. W2—3H 29
Orme La. W2—3H 29
Orme Sq. W2—3H 29
Ormond Clo. WC1—3H 23
Ormonde Ga. SW3—3B & 4B 56
Ormonde Pl. SW1—1E 57
Ormonde Ter. NW8—1B 8
Ormond M. WC1—2H 23
Ormond Yd. SW1—4B 34
Ormsby St. E2—2G 15
Orsett St. SE11—2B 60
Orsett Ter. W2—6A 18
Orsman Rd. N1—1E 15

Osbert St. SW1—1C 58
Oslo Ct. NW8—3H 7
Osnaburgh St. NW1—2H 21
Osnaburgh Ter. NW1—1H 21
Ossington Bldgs. W1—4E 21
Ossington Clo. W2—3G 29
Ossington St. W2—3G 29
Ossulston St. NW1—3D 10
Osten M. SW7—5A 42
Oswin St. SE11—5F 49
Othello Clo. SE11—2E 61
Otto St. SE11 & SE17—5E 61
Outer Circ. NW1—2A to 5A 8
Outwich St. EC3—5F 27
Oval Rd. NW1—1G 9
Oval Way. SE11—3A 60
Ovington Gdns. SW3—4H 43
Ovington M. SW3—4H 43
Ovington Sq. SW3—4A 44
Ovington St. SW3—5A 44
Owen's Ct. EC1—4E 13
Owen's Row. EC1—4E 13
Owen St. EC1—4E 13
Oxendon St. SW1—3D 34
Oxford Cir. W1—6H 21
Oxford Cir. Av. W1—6A 22
Oxford Ct. EC4—2B 38
Oxford Gdns. W10—5A 16
Oxford Rd. NW6—3G 5
Oxford Sq. W2—6H 19
Oxford St. W1—1C 32 to 6D 22

Packington Sq. N1—1H 13
Packington St. N1—1G to 2H 13
Padbury. SE17—3F 63
Paddington Grn. W2—4E 19
Paddington St. W1—4C 20
Page St. SW1—6D 46
Page's Wlk. SE1—6E 51
Paget St. EC1—4E 13
Painswick Ct. SE15—6H 63
Pakenham St. WC1—6B 12
Palace Av. W8—1A 42
Palace Ct. W2—3G 29
Palace Gdns. M. W8—4G 29
Palace Gdns. Ter. W8—4G 29
Palace Ga. SW7—2B 42
Palace Grn. W8—6H 29
Palace M. SW1—1E 57
Palace Pl. SW1—3H 45
Palace St. SW1—3A 46
Palissy St. E2—6H 15
 (in two parts)
Palliser Rd. W14—3A 52
Pall Mall. SW1—6B 34
Pall Mall E. SW1—4D 34
Pall Mall Pl. SW1—5B 34
Palmer St. SW1—3C to 4C 46
Pancras La. EC4—1B 38
Pancras Rd. NW1—2D 10
Panton St. SW1—3D 34
Panyer All. EC4—6H 25
Parade, The. SW11—6D 56
Paradise Wlk. SW3—4B 56
Paragon All. SE1—4E 51
Paragon M. SE1—5D 50
Paragon Row. SE17—6B 50
Pardoner St. SE1—3C 50
 (in two parts)
Pardon St. EC1—1G 25
Paris Garden. SE1—5E 37
Park Clo. SW1—1A 44
Park Clo. W14—3D 40
Park Cres. W1—2F 21
Park Cres. E. W1—2G 21
Park Cres. M. W. W1—2F 21
Parker M. WC2—6G 23
Parker St. WC2—6G 23
Parkfield St. N1—2D 12
Parkhouse St. SE5—6D 62
Park La. W1—2C 32
Park Pl. SW1—5A 34
Park Pl. Gdns. W2—3D 18
Park Pl. Vs. W2—3C 18
Park Rd.—5H 7 to 2B 20
 NW1 1-71 & 2-98
 NW8 remainder

Park Sq. E. NW1—1G 21
Park Sq. M. NW1—2F 21
Park Sq. W. NW1—1F 21
Park St. SE1—4H 37 to 5B 38
Park St. W1—2D 32
Park Village E. NW1—1G 9
Park Village W. NW1—2G 9
Park Wlk. SW10—4D 54
Parkway. NW1—1G 9
Park W. Pl. W2—6H 19
Parliament E. EC1—4G 27
Parliament Sq. SW1—2F 47
Parliament St. SW1—1F 47
Parr St. N1—2B 14
Parry St. SW8—5G 59
Partridge Ct. EC1—1F 25
Pasley Clo. SE17—3G 61
Passfields. W14—4B 52
Passing All. EC1—3F 25
Passmore St. SW1—1D 56
Pastor St. SE11—5G 49
Patchway Ct. SE15—6E 63
Paternoster Row. EC4—6H 25
Paternoster Sq. EC4—6G 25
Pater St. W8—4E 41
Paul St. EC2—2D 26
Paul's Wlk. EC4—2F 37
Paultons Sq. SW3—5F 55
Paulton St. SW3—5F 55
Paveley St. NW8—6H 7
Pavilion Rd. SW1—2B to 6C 44
Pavilion St. SW1—4C 44
Peabody Av. SW1—2G 57
Peabody Bldgs. EC1—2A 26
Peabody Bldgs. SE1—5H 37
Peabody Est. EC1—2D 24
Peabody Est. SE1—1A 50
Peabody Sq. SE1—2E 49
Peacock St. SE17—1G 61
Peacock Yd. SE17—1G 61
Pearman St. SE1—3D 48
Pear Pl. SE1—1C 48
Pearson St. E2—2G 15
Pear Tree Ct. EC1—2D 24
Pear Tree St. EC1—1G 25
Peel Pas. W8—5E 29
Peel Precinct. NW6—3E 5
Peel Rd. NW6—4D 4
Peel St. W8—6E 29
Peerless St. EC1—6B 14
Pegasus Pl. SE11—4C 60
Pelham Cres. SW7—1G 55
Pelham Pl. SW7—6F 43
Pelham St. SW7—6F 43
Pelier St. SE17—5A 62
Pellant Rd. SW6—6A 52
Pelter St. E2—4H 15
Pemberton Row. EC4—6D 24
Pembridge Cres. W11—2D 28
Pembridge Gdns. W2—3F 29
Pembridge M. W11—2E 29
Pembridge Pl. W2—2F 29
Pembridge Rd. W11—3E 29
Pembridge Sq. W2—3F 29
Pembridge Vs. W11—2E 29
Pembroke Clo. SW1—2E 45
Pembroke Gdns. W8—5D 40
Pembroke Gdns. Clo. W8—5D 40
Pembroke M. W8—4E 41
Pembroke Pl. W8—4E 41
Pembroke Rd. W8—6D 40 to 5F 41
Pembroke Sq. W8—5E 41
Pembroke Vs. W8—5E 41
Pembroke Wlk. W8—5E 41
Pencombe M. W11—2D 28
Penfold Pl. NW1—4H 19
Penfold St. NW8 & NW1—2E 19
Pennant M. W8—5H 41
Penn St. N1—1C 14
Pennymoor Wlk. W9—6D 4
Penrose Gro. SE17—3H 61
Penrose St. SE17—3H 61
Penryn Ho. SE11—2E 60
Penryn St. NW1—2D 10
Penry St. SE1—1F 63
Penton Gro. N1—3C 12
Penton Pl. SE17—1F 61
Penton Rise. WC1—4A 12

Penton St. N1—2C 12
Pentonville Rd. N1—4G 11
Penywern Rd. SW5—2G 53
Penzance Ho. SE11—2E 61
Penzance Pl. W11—4A 28
Penzance St. W11—5A 28
Pepper St. SE1—1H 49
Pepys St. EC3—2F 39
Percival St. EC1—6F 13
Percy Cir. WC1—5B 12
Percy M. W1—5C 22
Percy Pas. W1—5C 22
Percy Rd. NW6—4E 5
Percy St. W1—5C 22
Percy Yd. WC1—5B 12
Perham Rd. W14—4B 52
Perkin's Rents. SW1—4D 46
Perry's Pl. W1—6C 22
Peterborough Ct. EC4—6E 25
Petersham La. SW7—4B 42
Petersham M. SW7—4C 42
Petersham Pl. SW7—4C 42
Peters Hill. EC4—2H 37
Peter's La. EC1—3F 25
Peter St. W1—2C 34
Peto Pl. NW1—1G 21
Petticoat La. E1—5G 27
Petticoat Sq. E1—5G 27
Petty France. SW1—3B 46
Petyt Pl. SW3—6G 55
Petyward. SW3—1H 55
Phelp St. SE17—4C 62
Phene St. SW3—5H 55
Philbeach Gdns. SW5—2E 53
Phillimore Gdns. W8—2E 41
Phillimore Gdns. Clo. W8—3E 41
Phillimore Pl. W8—2E 41
Phillimore Ter. W8—3F 41
Phillimore Wlk. W8—3E 41
Phillipp St. N1—1E 15
Philpot La. EC3—2D 38
Phipp's M. SW1—5G 45
Phipp St. EC2—1E 27
Phoenix Ct. EC1—6F 25
Phoenix Pl. WC1—1B 24
Phoenix Rd. NW1—4C 10
Phoenix St. WC2—1E 35
Physic Pl. SW3—4B 56
Piazza, The. WC2—2G 35
Piccadilly. W1—6F 33 to 3C 34
Piccadilly Arc. SW1—4B 34
Piccadilly Cir. W1—3C 34
Piccadilly Pl. W1—3B 34
Pickard St. EC1—4G 13
Pickering M. W2—6H 17
Pickering Pl. SW1—5B 34
Pickwick St. SE1—2H 49
Picton Pl. W1—6E 21
Pierrepont Arc. N1—2E 13
Pierrepont Row. N1—2E 13
Pikemans Ct. SW5—1E 53
Pilgrimage St. SE1—2B 50
Pilgrim St. EC4—1F 37
Pimlico Rd. SW1—2D 56
Pimlico Wlk. N1—4E 15
Pindar St. EC2—3E 27
Pindock M. W9—2A 18
Pine Apple Ct. SW1—3B 46
Pine St. EC1—1C 24
Pitfield Est. N1—5E 15
Pitfield St. N1—6D 14 to 1E 15
Pitt's Ct. SE1—6E 39
Pitt's Head M. W1—5F 33
Pitt St. W8—1F 41
Plantain Pl. SE1—1C 50
Platina St. EC2—1D 26
Platt St. NW1—2D 10
Playhouse Yd. EC4—1F 37
Plender Pl. NW1—1B 10
Plender St. NW1—1A 10
Pleydell Est. EC1—6A 14
Pleydell St. EC4—1D 36
Plough Ct. EC3—2D 38
Plough Pl. EC4—5D 24
Plough Yd. EC2—2F 27
Plumtree Ct. EC4—5E 25
Plympton Pl. NW8—2G 19
Plympton St. NW8—2G 19

Pocock St. SE1—1F 49
Poet's Corner. SW1—3F 47
Poland St. W1—6B 22
Pollen St. W1—1H 33
Pollitt Dri. NW8—1E 19
Polygon Rd. NW1—4C 10
Pomell Way. E1—6H 27
Pond Pl. SW3—1G 55
Ponsonby Pl. SW1—2E 59
Ponsonby Ter. SW1—2E 59
Ponton Rd. SW8—6D 58
Pont St. SW1—4A 44
Pont St. M. SW1—4A 44
Pontypool Pl. SE1—1E 49
Pooles Bldgs. EC1—2C 24
Poole St. N1—1C 14
Pope's Head All. EC3—1C 38
Pope St. SE1—2G 51
Poplar Pl. W2—2H 29
Poppins Ct. EC4—6E 25
Porchester Gdns. M. W2—1A 30
Porchester Gnds. W2—1A 30
Porchester M. W2—6A 18
Porchester Pl. W2—6H 19
Porchester Sq. W2—5H 17
Porchester Sq. W2—6A 18
Porchester Ter. W2—1B 30
Porchester Ter. N. W2—6A 18
Porlock St. SE1—1C 50
Porter St. W1—3C 20
Porteus Rd. W2—4D 18
Portgate Clo. W9—1C 16
Porticos, The. SW3—5E 55
Portland M. W1—1C 34
Portland Pl. W1—3G 21
Portland Rd. W11—3A 28
Portland St. SE17—2B 62
Portland Wlk. SE17—5C 62
Portman Bldgs. NW1—2H 19
Portman Clo. W1—6C 20
Portman M. S. W1—1D 32
Portman Sq. W1—6D 20
Portman St. W1—1C 32
Portnall Rd. W9—4C 4
Portobello M. W11—3E 29
Portobello Rd.—4A 16 to 3E 29
  W11 1-275 & 2-262
  W10 remainder
Portpool La. EC1—3C 24
Portsea M. W2—1A 32
Portsea Pl. W2—6A 20
Portsmouth Bldgs. SE1—5E 51
Portsmouth St. WC2—6A 24
Portsoken St. E1—2H 39
Portugal St. WC2—1A 36
Postern, The. EC2—4A 26
Post Office Ct. EC3—1C 38
Post Office Way. SW8—6D 58
Potier St. SE1—4D 50
Potters' Fields. SE1—6F 39
Pottery La. W11—4A 28
Poultry. EC2—1B 38
Powis Gdns. W11—6C 16
Powis M. W11—6D 16
Powis Pl. WC1—3H 23
Powis Sq. W11—6D 16
Powis Ter. W11—6D 16
Praed M. W2—6F 19
Praed St. W2—1E 31
Pratt M. NW1—1A 10
Pratt St. NW1—1A 10
Pratt Wlk. SE11—5A 48
Prebend St. N1—1H 13
Prescot St. E1—2H 39
President St. EC1—5H 13
Preston Clo. SE1—6E 51
Prestwood St. N1—3A 14
Price's St. SE1—5F 37
Prideaux Pl. WC1—5B 12
Priest's Ct. EC2—6H 25
Prima Rd. SW9—6C 60
Primrose Hill. EC4—1E 37
Primrose St. EC2—3E 27
Prince Albert Rd.—4G 7 to 1F 9
  NW1 1-23
  NW8 remainder
Prince Consort Rd. SW7—3D 42
Princedale Rd. W11—4A 28

Princelet St. E1—3H 27
Prince of Wales Pas. NW1—5A 10
Prince of Wales Ter. W8—2A 42
Prince Regent Ct. NW8—2A 8
Princes Arc. SW1—4B 34
Princes Cir. WC2—6F 23
Prince's Gdns. SW7—3F 43
Prince's Ga. SW7—2F 43
  (in three parts)
Prince's Ga. Ct. SW7—2E 43
Prince's Ga. M. SW7—4F 43
Prince's M. W2—2G 29
Princes Pl. SW1—5B 34
Princes Pl. W11—5A 28
Prince's Sq. W2—2G 29
Princess Rd. NW6—3E 5
Princess St. SE1—4F 49
Princes St. EC2—6C 26
Princes St. W1—1H 33
Prince's Yd. W11—5A 28
Princeton St. WC1—4A 24
Printer St. EC4—6D 24
Printing Ho. Yd. E2—5G 15
Prioress St. SE1—4D 50
Priory Grn. Est. N1—2A 12
Priory Wlk. SW10—3C 54
Procter St. WC1—4H 23
Prothero Rd. SW6—6B 52
Providence Ct. W1—2E 33
Providence Row. N1—4H 11
Province St. N1—2H 13
Provost Est. N1—4C 14
Provost St. N1—5C to 4B 14
Prudent Pas. EC2—6B 26
Pudding La. EC3—3D 38
Puddle Dock. EC4—2F 37
Pulteney Ter. N1—1B 12
Puma Ct. E1—3H 27
Pump Ct. EC4—1C 36
Purbrook St. SE1—3F 51
Purcell St. N1—3E 15
Purchese St. NW1—2D 10

Quadrant Arc. W1—3B 34
Quadrant Ho. SE1—5F 37
Quaker St. E1—2G 27
Quality Ct. WC2—5C 24
Quebec M. W1—6C 20
Quedgeley Ct. SE15—6G 63
Queen Anne M. W1—5G 21
Queen Anne's Ga. SW1—2C 46
Queen Anne St. W1—5F 21
Queen Elizabeth St. SE1—6G 39 to 1H 51
Queenhithe. EC4—3A 38
Queensberry M. W. SW7—6D 42
Queensberry Pl. SW7—5D 42
Queensberry Way. SW7—6E 43
Queensborough M. W2—2B 30
Queensborough Pas. W2—2B 30
Queensborough Studios. W2—2B 30
Queensborough Ter. W2—2A 30
Queens Club Gdns. W14—5A 52
Queensdale Rd. W11—5A 28
Queen's Elm Sq. SW3—3E 55
Queen's Gdns. NW1—1A 46
Queen's Gdns. W2—2B 30
Queen's Ga. SW7—2C to 6D 42
Queen's Ga. Gdns. SW7—5C 42
Queen's Ga. M. SW7—3C 42
Queen's Ga. Pl. SW7—4C 42
Queen's Ga. Pl. M. SW7—5C 42
Queen's Ga. Ter. SW7—4B 42
Queen's Gro. NW8—1D 6
Queen's Head St. N1—1G 13
Queen's Head Yd. SE1—6B 38
Queen's M. W2—2H 29
Queen Sq. WC1—3G 23
Queen Sq. Pl. WC1—3G 23
Queen's Row. SE17—4B 62
Queen's Ter. NW8—1E 7
Queenstown Rd. SW8—5F 57
Queen St. EC4—2A 38
Queen St. W1—4G 33
Queen St. Pl. EC4—3A 38
Queen's Wlk. SW1—5A 34
Queensway. W2—6H 17 to 3A 30

Queen's Yd. WC1—3C 22
Queen Victoria St. EC4—2F 37
Quenington Ct. SE15—6G 63
Quick St. N1—3F 13
Quilp St. SE1—1H 49

Rabbit Row. W8—4F 29
Racton Rd. SW6—5E 53
Radcot St. SE11—3D 60
Raddington Rd. W10—4B 16
Radley M. W8—5G 41
Radnor M. W2—1F 31
Radnor Pl. W2—6F 19
Radnor Rd. NW6—1A 4
Radnor St. EC1—6A 14
Radnor Ter. W14—5C 40
Radnor Wlk. SW3—3A 56
Railway App. SE1—5C 38
Railway M. W10—6A 16
Railway St. N1—3G 11
Raleigh St. N1—1G 13
Ralston St. SW3—4B 56
Ramillies Pl. W1—6A 22
Ramillies St. W1—6A 22
Rampayne St. SW1—2D 58
Randall Rd. SE11—1H 59
Randall Row. SE11—1H 59
Randolph Av. W9—4H 5
Randolph Cres. W9—2B 18
Randolph Gdns. NW6—3G 5
Randolph M. W9—2C 18
Randolph Rd. W9—2C 18
Ranelagh Bri. W2—5A 18
Ranelagh Gro. SW1—2E 57
Ranelagh Rd. SW1—3B 58
Ranston St. NW1—3G 19
Raphael St. SW7—2A 44
Ratcliff Gro. EC1—6A 14
Rathbone Pl. W1—5C 22
Rathbone St. W1—5C 22
Ravenstone. SE17—3F 63
Ravensdon St. SE11—3D 60
Ravent Rd. SE11—6A 48
Ravey St. EC2—1E 27
Rawlings St. SW3—6A 44
Rawstorne Pl. EC1—5E 13
Rawstorne St. EC1—5E 13
Raymond Bldgs. WC1—3B 24
Ray St. EC1—2D 24
Ray St. Bri. EC1—2D 24
Rector St. N1—1H 13
Red Anchor Clo. SW3—5F 55
Redan Pl. W2—1H 29
Redburn St. SW3—4A 56
Redchurch St. E2—1G 27
Redcliffe Gdns. SW10—3H 53
Redcliffe M. SW10—3A 54
Redcliffe Pl. SW10—5B 54
Redcliffe Rd. SW10—4C 54
Redcliffe Sq. SW10—3H 53
Redcliffe St. SW10—4A 54
Redcross Way. SE1—1A 50 to 5B 38
Rede Pl. W2—1F 29
Redesdale St. SW3—4A 56
Redfield La. SW5—6G 41
Redhill St. NW1—4G 9
Red Lion Clo. SE17—5B 62
Red Lion Ct. EC4—6D 24
Red Lion Row. SE17—5B 62
Red Lion Sq. WC1—4H 23
Red Lion St. WC1—4A 24
Red Lion Yd. W1—5F 33
Red Pl. W1—2D 32
Redvers St. N1—4F 15
Reece M. SW7—6E 43
Reedworth St. SE11—1D 60
Rees St. N1—1B 14
Reeves M. W1—3D 32
Regal La. NW1—1F 9
Regan Way. N1—3E 15
Regency Pl. SW1—5D 46
Regency St. SW1—6D 46
Regent Pl. W1—3B 34
Regent's Bri. Gdns. SW8—6H 59
Regents M. NW8—3D 6
Regent's Pk. Est. NW1—5A 10
Regent Sq. WC1—6G 11

Regent St.—5H 21 to 4C 34
SW1 1-37 & 2-36
W1 remainder
Regnart Bldgs. NW1—6B 10
Relton M. SW7—3H 43
Rembrandt Clo. SW1—1D 56
Remington St. N1—4G 13
Remnant St. WC2—6H 23
Rempstone M. N1—2C 14
Renfrew Rd. SE11—6E 49
Rennie Ct. SE1—4E 37
Rennie St. SE1—4E 37
Reston Pl. SW7—2B 42
Retford St. N1—4F 15
Rex Pl. W1—4E 33
Rheidol M. N1—2G 13
Rheidol Ter. N1—2G 13
Rhoda St. E2—6H 15
Richardson's M. W1—2A 22
Richard's Pl. SW3—6H 43
Richbell Pl. WC1—3A 24
Rich La. SW5—3G 53
Richmond Bldgs. W1—1C 34
Richmond M. W1—1C 34
Richmond Ter. SW1—1F 47
Richmond Ter. M. SW1—1F 47
Rickett St. SW6—4F 53
Ridgmount Gdns. WC1—3C 22
Ridgmount Pl. WC1—4D 22
Ridgmount St. WC1—3D 22
Riding Ho. St. W1—5H 21 to 4B 22
Rifle Ct. SE11—4D 60
Riley Rd. SE1—3G 51
Riley St. SW10—6E 55
Ring, The. W2—5G 31.
Risborough St. SE1—6G 37
Risinghill St. N1—3B 12
Rising Sun Ct. EC1—4G 25
Rita Rd. SW8—6H 59
Ritchie St. N1—2D 12
Riverside Wlk. SE1—4B 36
(Lambeth)
Riverside Wlk. SE1—4F 37
(Southwark)
River St. EC1—5C 12
Riverton Clo. W9—6C 4
Rivington Pl. EC2—6F 15
Rivington St. EC2—6E 15
Robert Adam St. W1—5D 20
Robert Clo. W9—2D 18
Robert Dashwood Way. SE17—1H 61
Roberts M. SW1—4E 45
Roberts Pl. EC1—1D 24
Robert St. NW1—5H 9
Robert St. WC2—3G 35
Robinson St. SW3—5A 56
Rochelle St. E2—6H 15
(in two parts)
Rochester Row. SW1—6B 46
Rochester St. SW1—5C 46
Rochester Wlk. SE1—5B 38
Rockingham St. SE1—4H 49
Rocliffe St. N1—3G 13
Rodmarton St. W1—4C 20
Rodney Ct. W9—1D 18
Rodney Pl. SE17—5A 50
Rodney Rd. SE17—6B 50
Rodney St. N1—2B 12
Roger St. WC1—2A 24
Roland Gdns. SW7—2C to 3C 54
Roland Way. SE17—4C 62
Roland Way. SW7—2C 54
Rolls Bldgs. EC4—6D 24
Rolls Pas. EC4—6C 24
Roman Ho. EC2—4A 26
Romilly St. W1—2D 34
Romney St. SW1—5E 47
Rood La. EC3—2E 39
Ropemaker St. EC2—3B 26
Roper La. SE1—2F 51
Rosary Gdns. SW7—1C 54
Rose All. SE1—4A 38
Rosebery Av. EC1—2C 24
Rosebery Sq. EC1—2C 24
Roscoe St. EC1—2A 26
(in two parts)
Rose & Crown Ct. EC2—6H 25
Rose & Crown Yd. SW1—5B 34

Rosehart M. W11—1E 29
Rosemoor St. SW3—1A 56
Rose St. WC2—2F 35
Rosmead Rd. W11—2A 28
Rosoman Pl. EC1—6D 12
Rosoman St. EC1—6D 12
Rossmore Rd. NW1—2H 19
Rotary St. SE1—3F 49
Rotherham Wlk. SE1—6F 37
Rothsay St. SE1—4E 51
Rotten Row. SW7 & SW1—1F 43 to 1D 44
Roupell St. SE1—6D 36
Rowcross Pl. SE1—2H 63
Rowcross St. SE1—2H 63
Rowington Clo. W2—3H 17
Roxby Pl. SW6—4F 53
Royal Arc. W1—4A 34
Royal Av. SW3—2B 56
Royal College St. NW1—1C 10
Royal Exchange Av. EC3—1D 38
Royal Exchange Bldgs. EC3—1D 38
Royal Hospital Rd. SW3—5A 56
Royal Opera Arc. SW1—4D 34
Royal Rd. SE17—5E 61
Royal St. SE1—3A 48
Royalty M. W1—1D 34
Rudolph Rd. NW6—3G 5
Rufus St. N1—5E 15
Rugby St. WC1—3A 24
Rupert Ct. W1—2D 34
Rupert Rd. NW6—3D 4
Rupert St. W1—2C 34
Rushton St. N1—2C 14
Rushworth St. SE1—1F 49
Russell Ct. SW1—6B 34
Russell Gdns. W14—3A 40
Russell Rd. W14—3A 40
Russell Sq. WC1—2F 23
Russell St. WC2—2G 35
Russia Row. EC2—6A 26
Rutherford St. SW1—6D 46
Rutland Ct. EC1—2H 25
Rutland Gdns. SW7—2H 43
Rutland Gdns. M. SW7—2H 43
Rutland Ga. SW7—2H 43
Rutland Ga. M. SW7—3G 43
Rutland M. NW8—1A 6
Rutland M. E. SW7—3H 43
Rutland M. S. SW7—3H 43
Rutland Pl. EC1—3G 25
Rutland St. SW7—3H 43
Rutley Clo. SE17—5E 61
Ryde Bldgs. SE1—5E 51
Ryder Ct. SW1—5B 34
Ryder's Ter. NW8—2B 6
Ryder St. SW1—5B 34
Ryder Yd. SW1—5B 34
Rylston Rd. SW6—6B 52
Rysbrack St. SW3—3B 44

Sackville St. W1—3B 34
Saffron Hill. EC1—3D 24
Saffron St. EC1—3D 24
Sage Way. WC1—5A 12
Sail St. SE11—5B 48
St Agnes Pl. SE11—6E & 5E 61
St Agnes Well. EC1—6C 14
St Albans Ct. EC2—5A 26
St Alban's Gro. W8—3A 42
St Alban's M. W2—3F 19
St Alban's Pl. N1—1E 13
St Alban's St. SW1—4D 34
St Alphage Garden. EC2—4A 26
St Alphage Highwalk. EC2—5A 26
St Alphage Ho. EC2—4A 26
St Andrew's Hill. EC4—2F 37
St Andrew's M. NW1—1G 21
St Andrew's Rd. W14—4A 52
St Andrew St. EC4—5D 24
St Anne's Ct. W1—1C 34
St Ann's La. SW1—4D 46
St Ann's St. SW1—3E 47
St Ann's Ter. NW8—2F 7
St Anselm's Pl. W1—1F 33
St Barnabas St. SW1—2E 57
St Benet's Pl. EC3—2D 38
St Botolph Row. EC3—6G 27

St Botolph St. EC3—6G 27
St Briavel's Ct. SE15—6F 63
St Bride's Av. EC4—1E 37
St Bride's Pas. EC4—1E 37
St Bride St. EC4—6E 25
St Catherines M. SW3—6A 44
St Chad's Pl. WC1—4H 11
St Chad's St. WC1—5G & 4G 11
St Christopher's Pl. W1—6F 21
St Clare St. EC3—1H 39
St Clement's Ct. EC4—2D 38
St Clement's La. WC2—1A 26
St Cross St. EC1—3D 24
St Dunstan's All. EC3—3E 39
St Dunstan's Ct. EC4—6D 24
St Dunstan's Hill. EC3—3E 39
St Dunstan's La. EC3—3E 39
St Edmund's Clo. NW8—1B 8
St Edmund's Ter. NW8—1A 8
St Edward's Ct. SW8—5E 59
St Ermin's Hill. SW1—3C 46
St Ervan's Rd. W10—3B 16
St George's Bldgs. SE1—1A 50
St George's Cir. SE1—3F 49
St George's Dri. SW1—1H 57
St George's Fields. W2—1H 31
St George's La. EC3—3D 38
St George's Rd. SE1—3D 48
St George's Sq. SW1—2C to 3C 58
St George's Sq. M. SW1—3D 58
St George St. W1—1H 33
St George's Way. SE15—5E 63
St Giles Cir. W1, WC1 & WC2—6D 22
St Giles High St. WC2—6E 23
St Giles Pas. WC2—6E 23
St Helena St. WC1—5C 12
St Helen's Pl. EC3—6E 27
St James' Ct. SW1—3B 46
St James's App. EC2—2E 27
St James's Mkt. SW1—3D 34
St James's Pas. EC3—6G 27
St James's Pl. SW1—5A 34
St James's Row. EC1—1E 25
St James's Sq. SW1—4C 34
St James's St. SW1—5A 34
St James's Ter. NW8—1A 8
St James's Ter. M. NW8—1A 8
St James's Wlk. EC1—1E 25
St John's Est. N1—3D 14
St John's Est. SE1—1G 51
St John's Gdns. W11—4B 28
St John's La. EC1—3F 25
St John's M. W11—1E 29
St John's Path. EC1—3F 25
St John's Pl. EC1—2F 25
St John's Sq. EC1—2F 25
(in two parts)
St John St. EC1—4E 13 to 4F 25
St John's Wood Ct. NW8—6F 7
St John's Wood High St. NW8—3F 7
St John's Wood Pk. NW8—1E 7
St John's Wood Rd. NW8—1D 18
St John's Wood Ter. NW8—2F 7
St Joseph's Clo. W10—4B 16
St Katharine's Precinct. NW1—3F 9
St Katharine's Way. E1—4H 39
St Katherine's Row. EC3—1F 39
St Lawrence Ter. W10—4A 16
St Leonard's Ct. N1—4D 14
St Leonard's Ter. SW3—3B 56
St Loo Av. SW3—5A 56
St Luke's Clo. EC1—1A 26
St Luke's Est. EC1—6B 14
St Luke's M. W11—6C 16
St Lukes Rd. W11—5C 16
St Luke's St. SW3—2H 55
St Luke's Yd. W9—4B 4
St Margaret's Ct. SE1—6B 38
St Margaret's St. SW1—2F 47
St Mark's Gro. SW10—6A 54
St Mark's Pl. W11—1A 28
St Mark's Rd. W11—1A 28
St Martin's Ct. WC2—2E 35
St Martin's La. WC2—2F 35
St Martin's le Grand. EC1—6H 25
St Martin's Pl. WC2—3F 35
St Martin's St. WC2—3E 35
St Martins Wlk. SE1—5D 37

St Mary Abbot's Pl. W8—5D 40
St Mary Abbot's Ter. W14—4C 40
St Mary at Hill. EC3—3E 39
St Mary Axe. EC3—6F 27
St Mary's Gdns. SE11—6D 48
St Mary's Mans. W2—3D 18
St Mary's Sq. W2—4D 18
St Mary's Ter. W2—3D 18
St Mary's Wlk. SE11—6D 48
St Matthew St. SW1—4D 46
St Michael's All. EC3—1D 38
St Michael's St. W2—6F 19
St Mildred's Ct. EC2—1C 38
St Olaf Ho. SE1—5D 38
St Olaf Stairs. SE1—5D 38
St Olave's Ct. EC2—6B 26
St Olave's Gdns. SE11—6C 48
St Olave's Ter. SE1—6F 39
St Oswald's Pl. SE11—3A 60
St Oswulf St. SW1—1E 59
St Pancras Way. NW1—1C 10
St Paul's All. EC4—6G 25
St Paul's Chyd. EC4—1G 37
St Paul's Shopping Centre. EC4—6H 25
St Pauls Ter. SE17—4F 61
St Paul St. N1—1H 13 & 1A 14
St Peter's All. EC3—1D 38
St Petersburgh M. W2—2H 29
St Petersburgh Pl. W2—3H 29
St Peter's St. N1—1F 13
St Peter's St. M. N1—2G 13
St Saviour's Est. SE1—3G 51
St Stephen's Clo. NW8—1H 7
St Stephen's Cres. W2—5F 17
St Stephen's Gdns. W2—5E 17
St Stephen's M. W2—5F 17
St Stephen's Row. EC4—1C 38
St Stephen's Wlk. SW7—5B 42
St Swithin's La. EC4—2C 38
St Thomas St. SE1—5C 38
St Thomas's Way. SW6—6D 52
St Vincent St. W1—5E 21
Salamanca Pl. SE1—1H 59
Salamanca St. SE1 & SE11—1H 59
Salem Rd. W2—2H 29
Sale Pl. W2—5G 19
Salisbury Clo. SE17—6C 50
Salisbury Ct. EC4—1E 37
Salisbury Pl. W1—3B 20
Salisbury Sq. EC4—1E 37
Salisbury St. NW8—2F 19
Saltash Ho. SE11—2E 61
Salters Ct. EC4—1A 38
Salter's Hall Ct. EC4—2C 38
Saltram Cres. W9—4C 4
Saltwood Gro. SE17—3B 62
Salusbury Rd. NW6—1B 4
Samford St. NW8—2F 19
Samuel Lewis Trust Dwellings. SW3
                                —1G 55
Sancroft St. SE11—2B 60
Sanctuary St. SE1—1A 50
Sanctuary, The. SW1—3E 47
Sandell St. SE1—6C 36
Sandland St. WC1—4A 24
Sandringham Ct. W9—6C 6
Sandwich St. WC1—6F 11
Sandys Row. E1—4F 27
Sans Wlk. EC1—1E 25
Saperton Wlk. SE11—6B 48
Saracen's Head Yd. EC3—1G 39
Sarah St. N1—5F 15
Sardinia St. WC2—6A 24
Saul Ct. SE15—6G 63
Saunders St. SE11—6B 48
Savage Gdns. EC3—2G 39
Savile Row. W1—2A 34
Savoy Bldgs. WC2—3H 35
Savoy Ct. WC2—3H 35
Savoy Hill. WC2—3H 35
Savoy Pl. WC2—4G 35
Savoy Row. WC2—3H 35
Savoy Steps. WC2—3H 35
Savoy St. WC2—2H 35
Savoy Way. WC2—3H 35
Sawyer St. SE1—1G 49
Scala St. W1—4B 22
Scarsdale Pl. W8—3G 41

Scarsdale Vs. W8—5F 41
School App. E2—5F 15
Sclater St. E1—1H 27
Scoresby St. SE1—6F 37
Scotland Pl. SW1—5F 35
Scotswood St. EC1—1E 25
Scott Ellis Gdns. NW8—6D 7
Scott's Yd. EC4—2C 38
Scovell Cres. SE1—2H 49
Scovell Rd. SE1—2G 49
Scrutton St. EC2—2D 26
Seacoal La. EC4—6F 25
Seaford St. WC1—6H 11
Seaforth Pl. SW1—3B 46
Seagrave Rd. SW6—4F 53
Searles Rd. SE1—5C 50
Seaton Clo. SE11—2E 61
Seaton Pl. NW1—1A 22
Sebastian St. EC1—6F 13
Secker St. SE1—6C 36
Second Av. W10—1B 16
Sedan Way. SE17—2D 62
Sedding St. SW1—6D 44
Seddon Ho. EC2—4H 25
Seddon St. WC1—6A 12
Sedgwick Centre. E1—6H 27
Sedlescombe Rd. SW6—5D 52
Sedley Pl. W1—1F 33
Seething La. EC3—2F 39
Sekforde St. EC1—2E 25
Sellon M. SE11—1A 60
Selwood Rd. SW7—2E 55
Selwood Ter. SW7—2E 55
Semley Pl. SW1—1F 57
Senior St. W2—4H 17
Serjeant's Inn. EC4—1D 36
Serle St. WC2—6B 24
Sermon La. EC4—1G 37
Serpentine Rd. W2—5E 31
Setchell Rd. SE1—6H 51
Setchell Way. SE1—5G 51
Seven Dials. WC2—1F 35
Seven Dials Ct. WC2—1F 35
Seville St. SW1—2C 44
Sevington St. W9—2G 17
Seward St. EC1—6G 13
Seymour Clo. EC1—2E 25
Seymour M. W1—6D 20
Seymour Pl. W1—4A 20
Seymour St.—1A 32
  W1 1-61 & 2-68
  W2 remainder
Seymour Wlk. SW10—4B 54
Shad Thames. SE1—6G 39 & 2H 51
Shaftesbury Av.—3C 34
  W1 1-111 & 2-136
  WC2 remainder
Shaftesbury M. W8—5F 41
Shaftesbury St. N1—3B 14
Shafto M. SW1—5B 44
Shafts Ct. EC3—1E 39
Shakespeare Tower. EC2—3A 26
Shalcomb St. SW10—6D 54
Shalford St. N1—2F 13
Shand St. SE1—1E 51
Shannon Pl. NW8—2H 7
Shap St. E2—1G & 2G 15
Sharpness Ct. SE15—6G 63
Sharsted St. SE17—4E 61
Shaver's Pl. SW1—3D 34
Shawfield St. SW3—3H 55
Sheba St. E1—2H 27
Sheffield St. WC2—1A 36
Sheffield Ter. W8—6E 29
Sheldrake Pl. W8—1D 40
Shelton St. WC2—1F 35 to 6G 23
Shenfield St. N1—3F 15
Shepherdess Pl. N1—5B 14
Shepherdess Wlk. N1—2A 14
Shepherd Mkt. W1—5G 33
Shepherds Pl. W1—2D 32
Shepherd's Av. W1—5F 33
Sheraton St. W1—6C 22
Sherborne La. EC4—2C 38
Sherlock M. W1—3C 20
Sherston Ct. WC1—6C 12
Sherwood St. W1—3C 34
Shillibeer Pl. W1—4A 20

Ship & Mermaid Row. SE1—1D 50
Ship Tavern Pas. EC3—1D 38
Shirland M. W9—6D 4
Shirland Rd. W9—5C 4 to 2A 18
Shoe La. EC4—5E 25
Shoreditch High St. E1—6F 15
Shorncliffe Rd. SE1—3G 63
Shorter St. E1—3H 39
Shorts Gdns. WC2—1F 35
Short St. SE1—1E 49
Shouldham St. W1—5A 20
Shrewsbury M. W2—5E 17
Shrewsbury Rd. W2—5E 17
Shropshire Pl. WC1—2C 22
Shroton St. NW1—3H 19
Shuters Sq. W14—4C 52
Sicilian Av. WC1—4H 23
Siddons La. NW1—2B 20
Sidford Pl. SE1—4B 48
Sidmouth St. WC1—6H 11
Sidney Gro. EC1—4F 13
Silbury St. N1—5C 14
Silex St. SE1—2F 49
Silk St. EC2—3B 26
Silver Pl. W1—1C 34
Silvester St. SE1—2B 50
Simon Clo. W11—2D 28
Sinclair Rd. W14—4A 40
Singer St. EC2—6D 14
Sise La. EC4—1B 38
Skinner Pl. SW1—1D 56
Skinners La. EC4—2A 38
Skinner St. EC1—6D 12
Skipton St. SE1—4G 49
Slade Wlk. SE17—5G 61
Slaidburn St. SW10—6C 54
Slingsby Pl. WC2—2F 35
Sloane Av. SW3—6H 43
Sloane Ct. E. SW3—2D 56
Sloane Ct. W. SW3—2C 56
Sloane Gdns. SW1—1D 56
Sloane Sq. SW1—1C 56
Sloane St. SW1—2B 44
Sloane Ter. SW1—6C 44
Smallbrook M. W2—1D 30
Smart's Pl. WC2—5G 23
Smithfield St. EC1—5F 25
Smith's Ct. W1—2C 34
Smith Sq. SW1—4F 47
Smith St. SW3—2A 56
Smith Ter. SW3—3A 56
Smyrk's Rd. SE17—3F 63
Snowden St. EC2—3E 27
Snow Hill. EC1—5E 25
Snow Hill Ct. EC1—5F 25
Snowsfields. SE1—1D 50
Soho Sq. W1—6D 22
Soho St. W1—6D 22
Soley M. WC1—4C 12
Somers Clo. NW1—3D 10
Somers Cres. W2—6G 19
Somerset Sq. W14—3B 40
Somers M. W2—6G 19
S. Audley St. W1—3E 33
S. Bank Technopark. SE1—4F 49
S. Bolton Gdns. SW5—2A 54
S. Carriage Dri. SW7 & SW1
                          —2F 43 to 1E 45
Southcombe St. W14—6A 40
South Cres. WC1—4D 22
S. Eaton Pl. SW1—6E 45
S. Edwarde's Sq. W8—5D 40
S. End. W8—3H 41
S. End Row. W8—3H 41
Southern Row. W10—2A 16
Southern St. N1—3H 11
S. Kensington Sta. Arc. SW7—6F 43
S. Lambeth Pl. SW8—4G 59
S. Lambeth Rd. SW8—6G 59
S. Molton La. W1—1F 33
S. Molton St. W1—1F 33

South Pde. SW3—3E 55
South Pl. EC2—4C 26
South Pl. M. EC2—4C 26
South Sq. WC1—4C 24
South St. W1—4E 33
South Ter. SW7—6G 43
Southwark Bri. SE1 & EC4—4A 38
Southwark Bri. Rd. SE1—3G 49
Southwark Gro. SE1—6H 37
Southwark St. SE1—5F 37
Southwell Gdns. SW7—5B 42
S. Wharf Rd. W2—6E 19
Southwick M. W2—6E 19
Southwick Pl. W2—1G 31
Southwick St. W2—6G 19
Southwold Mans. W9—6F 5
Sovereign M. E2—2G 15
Spafield St. EC1—6C 12
Spa Grn. Est. EC1—5E 13
Spanish Pl. W1—5E 21
Spa Rd. SE16—4H 51
Sparrick's Row. SE1—6D 38
Speaker's Corner. W2—2C 32
Spear M. SW5—1F 53
Speed Ho. EC2—4B 26
Speedy Pl. WC1—6F 11
Spencer St. EC1—5E 13
Spenser St. SW1—4B 46
Spital Sq. E1—3F 27
Spital Yd. E1—3F 27
Sprimont Pl. SW3—2A 56
Springfield La. NW6—1G 5
Springfield Rd. NW8—1B 6
Springfield Wlk. NW6—1G 5
Spring Gdns. SW1—5E 35
Spring M. W1—4C 20
Spring St. W2—1E 31
Spurgeon St. SE1—4B 50
Spur Rd. SW1—2A 46
Stables Way. SE11—2C 60
Stable Yd. SW1—6A 34
Stable Yd. Rd. SW1—6B 34
Stacey St. WC2—1E 35
Stackhouse St. SW3—3B 44
Stafford Clo. NW6—5E 5
Stafford Pl. SW1—3A 46
Stafford Rd. NW6—4E 5
Stafford St. W1—4A 34
Stafford Ter. W8—3E 41
Staff St. EC1—6D 14
Stag Pl. SW1—4A 46
Stainer St. SE1—6D 38
Staining La. EC2—5A 26
Stalbridge St. NW1—3H 19
Stamford St. SE1—5C 36
Stamp Pl. E2—4H 15
Standard Pl. EC2—6F 15
Stanford Pl. SE17—1E 63
Stanford Rd. W8—3A 42
Stanford St. SW1—1C 58
Stanhope Gdns. SW7—6C 42
Stanhope Ga. W1—5E 33
Stanhope M. E. SW7—6D 42
Stanhope M. S. SW7—6C 42
Stanhope M. W. SW7—6C 42
Stanhope Pde. NW1—4A 10
Stanhope Pl. W2—1A 32
Stanhope Row. W1—5F 33
Stanhope St. NW1—4A 10 to 1A 22
Stanhope Ter. W2—2E 31
Stanier Clo. W14—3D 52
Stanley Clo. SW8—6H 59
Stanley Cres. W11—2C 28
Stanley Gdns. W11—2C 28
Stanley Gdns. M. W11—2C 28
Stanley Pas. NW1—3F 11
Stannary Pl. SE11—4D 60
Stannary St. SE11—4D 60
Stanway Ct. N1—3F 15
Stanway St. N1—2F 15
Stanwick Rd. W14—1B 52
Stanworth St. SE1—3H 51
Staple Inn. WC1—5C 24
Staple Inn Bldgs. WC1—5C 24
Staple St. SE1—3C 50
Star All. EC3—2F 39
Starcross St. NW1—6B 10
Star Rd. W14—4B 52

Star St. W2—6F 19
Star Yd. WC2—6C 24
Stationers' Hall Ct. EC4—1F 37
Steadman Ct. EC1—1A 26
Stead St. SE17—1B 62
Stedham Pl. WC1—5F 23
Steedman St. SE17—1H 61
Stephen M. W1—5C 22
Stephenson Way. NW1—6B 10
Stephen St. W1—5D 22
Sterling St. SW7—5B 44
Sterry St. SE1—2B 50
Stevens St. SE1—3F 51
Steward St. E1—4G 27
Stewart's Gro. SW3—1F 55
Stew La. EC4—2H 37
Stillington St. SW1—5B 46
Stone Bldgs. WC2—5B 24
Stonecutter St. EC4—6E 25
Stone Ho. Ct. EC3—5F 27
Stones End St. SE1—2H 49
Stoney La. E1—6G 27
Stoney St. SE1—5B 38
Stonor Rd. W14—1C 52
Stopford Rd. SE17—3G 61
Store St. WC1—4D 22
Storey's Ga. SW1—2E 47
Stothard Pl. EC2—3F 27
Stoughton Clo. SE11—1A 60
Stourcliffe St. W1—6A 20
Strand. WC2—4F 35 to 1C 36
Strand La. WC2—2B 36
Strangways Ter. W14—4C 40
Stratford Av. W8—4G 41
Stratford Pl. W1—6F 21
Stratford Rd. W8—5F 41
Strathearn Pl. W2—1F 31
Strathmore Gdns. W8—5F 29
Stratton St. W1—4H 33
Streatham St. WC1—5E 23
Strouts Pl. E2—4H 15
Strutton Ground. SW1—4C 46
Strype St. E1—5G 27
Stuart Rd. NW6—6E 5
Studio Pl. SW1—2C 44
Stukeley St. WC2—6G 23
Sturgeon Rd. SE17—3G 61
Sturge St. SE1—1G 49
Sturt St. N1—3A 14
Sudeley St. N1—3F 13
Sudrey St. SE1—2H 49
Suffolk La. EC4—2C 38
Suffolk Pl. SW1—4D 34
Suffolk St. SW1—4D 34
Sugar Baker's Ct. EC3—6F 27
Sugar Loaf Ct. EC4—2A 38
Sulivan Rd. SE1—6E 49
Summerfield Av. NW6—2B 4
Summers St. EC1—2C 24
Sumner Bldgs. SE1—5H 37
Sumner Pl. SW7—1E 55
Sumner Pl. M. SW7—1E 55
Sumner Rd. SE15—5H 63
Sumner St. SE1—5G 37
Sun Ct. EC3—1D 38
Sunderland Ter. W2—6G 17
Sunningdale Gdns. W8—5F 41
Sun Rd. W14—3C 52
Sun St. EC2—3D 26
Surrendale Pl. W9—2G 17
Surrey Gro. SE17—3E 63
Surrey Row. SE1—1F 49
Surrey Sq. SE17—2E 63
Surrey St. WC2—2B 36
Surrey Ter. SE17—1F 63
Sussex Gdns. W2—2E 31 to 5H 19
Sussex M. E. W2—2F 31
Sussex M. W. W2—2E 31
Sussex Pl. NW1—1B 20
Sussex Pl. W2—1F 31
Sussex Sq. W2—2F 31
Sussex St. SW1—3H 57
Sutherland Av. W9—2G 17 to 6C 6
Sutherland Pl. W2—6E 17
Sutherland Row. SW1—2G 57
Sutherland Sq. SE17—4H 61
Sutherland St. SW1—2G 57
Sutherland Wlk. SE17—3A 62

Sutton Est., The. SW3—2H 55
Sutton Row. W1—6D 22
Sutton's Way. EC1—2A 26
Swallow Pas. W1—6H 21
Swallow Pl. W1—1H 33
Swallow St. W1—3B 34
Swan Ct. SW3—4H 55
Swanfield St. E2—5H 15
Swan La. EC4—3C 38
Swan Mead. SE1—5E 51
Swan St. SE1—3A 50
Swan Wlk. SW3—5B 56
Sweeney Cres. SE1—2H 51
Swinbrook Rd. W10—3A 16
Swinton Pl. WC1—5A 12
Swinton St. WC1—5H 11
Sycamore St. EC1—2H 25
Sydney Clo. SW3—1F 55
Sydney M. SW3—1F 55
Sydney Pl. SW7—1F 55
Sydney St. SW3—1F 55
Symes M. NW1—2A 10
Symons St. SW3—1C 56

Tabard Garden Est. SE1—3C 50
Tabard St. SE1—1B to 4D 50
Tabernacle St. EC2—2C 26
Tachbrook Est. SW1—3D 58
Tachbrook M. SW1—6A 42
Tachbrook St. SW1—1B 58
Talbot Ct. EC3—2D 38
Talbot Rd. W11 & W2—6C & 6D 16
Talbot Sq. W2—1E 31
Talbot Yd. SE1—6B 38
Talgarth Rd. W14—2A 52
Tallis St. EC4—2D 36
Tamworth St. SW6—5E 53
Tankerton St. WC1—5G 11
Tanner St. SE1—2F to 2G 51
Taplow. SE17—2D 62
Taplow St. N1—3A 14
Tarn St. SE1—4H 49
Tarver Rd. SE17—3G 61
Tatum St. SE17—1D 62
Taunton M. NW1—2B 20
Taunton Pl. NW1—1A 20
Tavistock Cres. W11—5B & 4D 16
Tavistock Ho. WC1—6E 11
Tavistock M. W11—6B 16
Tavistock Pl. WC1—1E 23
Tavistock Rd. W11—5B 16
Tavistock Sq. WC1—1E 23
Tavistock St. WC2—2G to 1H 35
Taviton St. WC1—1D 22
Tavy Clo. SE11—2D 60
Tay Bldgs. SE1—3E 51
Tedworth Gdns. SW3—4A 56
Tedworth Sq. SW3—3A 56
Telegraph St. EC2—6C 26
Telephone Pl. SW6—5D 52
Telford Rd. W10—3A 16
Temple Av. EC4—2D 36
Temple La. EC4—1D 36
Temple Pl. WC2—2B 36
Templeton Pl. SW5—6F 41
Temple W. M. SE11—4F 49
Tenison Ct. W1—2A 34
Tenison Way. SE1—6B 36
Tenniel Clo. W2—2A 30
Tennis St. SE1—1B 50
Tennyson Rd. NW6—1C 4
Tenterden St. W1—1G 33
Tenter Ground. E1—4G 27
Terminus Pl. SW1—5H 45
Terrace, The. EC4—1D 36
Terrace, The. SW1—3G 47
Terrace Wlk. SW11—6B 56
Tetbury Pl. N1—1E 13
Thackeray St. W8—3H 41
Thanet St. WC1—6F 11
Thavies Inn. EC1—5D 24
Thaxton Rd. W14—4D 52
Thayer St. W1—5E 21
Theed St. SE1—6D 36
Theobald's Rd. WC1—4H 23
Theobald St. SE1—5C 50
Theseus Wlk. N1—3G 13

83

Waldron M. SW3—5F 55
Walham Gro. SW6—6F 53
Walham Yd. SW6—6E 53
Walker's Ct. W1—2C 34
Wallgrave Rd. SW5—6G 41
Wallgrave Ter. SW5—6G 41
Wallis All. SE1—1A 50
Walmer Pl. W1—4A 20
Walmer St. W1—4A 20
Walnut Tree Wlk. SE11—5C 48
Walpole St. SW3—2B 56
Walterton Rd. W9—2D 16
Walton St. SW3—4B 44
Walton St. SW3—6H 43
Walworth Pl. SE17—3A 62
Walworth Rd.—6G 49
  SE1 2-96
  SE17 remainder
Wandsworth Rd. SW8—6F 59
Wansey St. SE1—6H 37
Wardens Gro. SE1—6H 37
Wardour M. W1—1C 34
Wardour St. W1—6C 22
Wardrobe Pl. EC4—1G 37
Wardrobe Ter. EC4—2G 37
Warlock Rd. W9—1D 16 & 1E 17
Warmley Ct. SE15—6F 63
Warner St. EC1—2C 24
Warner Yd. EC1—2C 24
Warren M. W1—2H 21
Warren St. W1—2H 21
Warrington Cres. W9—2B 18
Warrington Gdns. W9—2A 18
Warwick Av.—2H 17 to 3C 18
  W2 4-16
  W9 remainder
Warwick Ct. WC1—4B 24
Warwick Cres. W2—4B 18
Warwick Est. W2—4H 17
Warwick Gdns. W14—5C 40
Warwick Ho. St. SW1—4D 34
Warwick Pl. W9—3B 18
Warwick Pl. N. SW1—1A 58
Warwick Rd.—5C 40 to 3G 53
  SW5 1-127 & 2-76
  W14 remainder
Warwick Row. SW1—4H 45
Warwick Sq. EC4—6F 25
Warwick Sq. SW1—2A 58
Warwick Sq. M. SW1—1A 58
Warwick St. W1—2B 34
Warwick Way. SW1—2G 57
Warwick Yd. EC1—2A 26
Watergate. EC4—2E 37
Watergate Wlk. WC2—4G 35
Waterloo Bri. WC2 & SE1—3A 36
Waterloo Pl. SW1—4D to 5D 34
Waterloo Rd. SE1—4B 36 to 3E 49
Waterson St. E2—5G 15
Water St. WC2—2B 36
Watling Ct. EC4—1A 38
Watling St. EC4—1H 37
Watson's M. W1—5H 19
Waverley Pl. NW8—2D 6
Waverton St. W1—4F 33
Waxwell Ter. SE1—2B 48
Weaver's La. SE1—6F 39
Weavers Ter. SW6—6F 53
Webber Row. SE1—2E 49
Webber St. SE1—1D 48 to 2G 49
Webb St. SE1—4E 51
Wedgwood M. W1—1D 34
Wedlake St. W10—1B 16
Weighhouse St. W1—1F 33
Weir's Pas. NW1—5E 11
Welbeck St. W1—5F 21
Welbeck Way. W1—5F 21
Well Ct. EC4—1A 38
Wellers Ct. N1—3F 11
Weller St. SE1—1H 49
Wellesley Ct. W9—5B 6
Wellesley Pl. NW1—5D 10
Wellesley Ter. N1—4A 14
Wellington Bldgs. SW1—3F 57
Wellington Clo. W11—1E 29
Wellington Ct. NW8—3E 7
Wellington Pl. NW8—4F 7

Wellington Rd. NW8—3E 7
Wellington Sq. SW3—2B 56
Wellington St. WC2—2H 35
Wellington Ter. W2—4G 29
Wellside. EC2—4A 26
Wells M. W1—5B 22
Wells Rise. NW8—1A 8
Wells Sq. WC1—6A 12
Wells St. W1—5A 22
Wells Way. SE5—5D 62
Wells Way. SW7—4D 42
Wendover. SE17—3D 62 & 3E 63
  (in two parts)
Wenlock Barn Est. N1—3C 14
Wenlock Rd. N1—3H 13
Wenlock St. N1—3A 14
Wentworth Mkt. E1—5G 27
Wentworth St. E1—5G 27
Werrington St. NW1—3C 10
Wesley Clo. SE17—1F 61
Wesley St. W1—4E 21
Westbourne Bri. W2—5B 18
Westbourne Cres. W2—2D 30
Westbourne Cres. M. W2—2D 30
Westbourne Gdns. W2—6H 17
Westbourne Gro.—2C 28 to 1H 29
  W2 1-131 & 2-112
  W11 remainder
Westbourne Gro. M. W11—1E 29
Westbourne Gro. Ter. W2—6H 17
Westbourne Pk. M. W2—6H 17
Westbourne Pk. Pas. W2—4G 17
Westbourne Pk. Rd.—6A 16 to 5H 17
  W2 1-139 & 2-150
  W11 remainder
Westbourne Pk. Vs. W2—5F 17
Westbourne Rd. Bri. W2 & W9—4B 18
Westbourne St. W2—2E 31
Westbourne Ter. W2—5B 18 to 4D 30
Westbourne Ter. M. W2—6B 18
Westbourne Ter. Rd. W2—4B 18
Westbourne Ter. Rd. Bri. W2—4B 18
W. Carriage Dri. W2—4G 31
W. Central St. WC1—5F 23
Westcott Rd. SE17—4F 61
W. Cromwell Rd. W14 & SW5—2C 52
W. Eaton Pl. SW1—6D 44
W. Eaton Pl. M. SW1—5D 44
Western Ct. W9—4C 4
Western M. W9—2D 16
W. Garden Pl. W2—6H 19
Westgate Ter. SW10—4H 53
W. Halkin St. SW1—3D 44
W. Harding St. EC4—6D 24
Westland Pl. N1—5B 14
W. Mall. W8—4F 29
West M. SW1—1H 57
Westminster Bri. SW1 & SE1—2G 47
Westminster Bri. Rd. SE1—2A 48 to 3E 49
Westmoreland Pl. SW1—3H 57
Westmoreland Rd. SE17—4B 62
Westmoreland St. W1—4F 21
Westmoreland Ter. SW1—3G 57
Westmoreland Wlk. SE17—5C 62
Westonbirt Ct. SE15—6H 63
West One Shopping Centre. W1—1F 33
Weston Rise. WC1—4A 12
Weston St. SE1—4D 50 to 5D 38
W. Poultry Av. EC1—4F 25
West Rd. SW3—4C 56
W. Smithfield. EC1—4F 25
West Sq. SE11—5E 49
West St. WC2—1E 35
W. Warwick Pl. SW1—1H 57
Westway. W10, W9 & W2—6A 16 to 4E 19
Wetherby Gdns. SW5—1B 54
Wetherby M. SW5—2H 53
Wetherby Pl. SW7—1C 54
Weymouth M. W1—4G 21
Weymouth St. W1—4E 21
Weymouth Ter. E2—1H & 3H 15
Whalebone Ct. EC2—6C 26
Wharfdale Rd. N1—2G 11
Wharfedale St. SW10—3H 53
Wharf Rd. N1—3H 13
Wharton Cotts. WC1—5B 12
Wharton St. WC1—5B 12
Wheatley St. W1—4E 21

Wheler St. E1—2G 27
Whetstone Pk. WC2—5A 24
Whichcote St. SE1—6C 36
Whidborne St. WC1—5G 11
Whiskin St. EC1—6E 13
Whiston Rd. E2—2G 15
Whitby St. E1—1H 27
Whitcomb St. WC2—3D 34
Whitcomb St. WC2—3D 34
Whitechapel High St. E1—6H 27
White Conduit St. N1—2D 12
  (in two parts)
Whitecross Pl. EC2—3D 26
Whitecross St. EC1 & EC2—1A 26
Whitefriars St. EC4—1D 36
Whitehall. SW1—5F 35
Whitehall Ct. SW1—6G 35
Whitehall Gdns. SW1—6F 35
Whitehall Pl. SW1—5F 35
White Hart Ct. EC2—5E 27
White Hart St. SE11—2D 60
White Hart Yd. SE1—6C 38
Whitehaven St. NW8—2G 19
Whitehead's Gro. SW3—2H 55
White Horse All. EC1—3F 25
Whitehorse M. SE1—3E 49
White Horse St. W1—5G 33
White Horse Yd. EC2—5B 26
White Kennett St. E1—6G 27
Whiteley's Cotts. W14—1C 52
White Lion Ct. EC3—1D 38
White Lion Hill. EC4—2G 37
White Lion St. N1—3C 12
White Lyon Ct. EC2—3H 25
White's Grounds. SE1—1F 51
White's Grounds Est. SE1—1F 51
White's Row. E1—4G 27
Whitfield Pl. W1—2B 22
Whitfield St. W1—2A 22
Whitgift St. SE11—6H 47
Whitminster St. SE15—6F 63
Whitmore Rd. N1—1E 15
Whittaker St. SW1—1D 56
Whittington Av. EC3—1E 39
Whittlesey St. SE1—6D 36
Wickham St. SE11—2A 60
Wicklow St. WC1—4H 11
Wickway Ct. SE15—6H 63
Widegate St. E1—4F 27
Widley Rd. W9—6F 5
Wigmore Pl. W1—5G 21
Wigmore St. W1—6D 20
Wigton Pl. SE11—3D 60
Wilbraham Pl. SW1—6C 44
Wilby M. W11—4C 28
Wilcox Pl. SW1—4B 46
Wild Ct. WC2—6H 23
Wild's Rents. SE1—3D 50
Wild St. WC2—6H 23
Wilfred St. SW1—3A 46
Wilkes St. E1—4H & 2H 27
Wilks Pl. N1—3F 15
William Cobbett Ho. W8—3G 41
William IV St. WC2—3F 35
William M. SW1—2C 44
William Rd. NW1—6H 9
William St. SW1—2C 44
Willoughby Ho. EC2—4B 26
Willoughby St. WC1—5F 23
Willow Ct. EC2—6D 14
Willow Pl. SW1—6B 46
Willow St. EC2—6D 14
Willow Wlk. SE1—5F 51
Wilmer Gdns. N1—1E & 1F 15
Wilmington Sq. WC1—6C 12
Wilmington St. WC1—6C 12
Wilson St. EC2—4D 26
Wilton Cres. SW1—2D 44
Wilton M. SW1—3F 45
Wilton Pl. SW1—2D 44
Wilton Rd. SW1—5H 45 to 6A 46
Wilton Row. SW1—2D 44
Wilton St. SW1—4F 45
Wilton Ter. SW1—3D 44
Wiltshire Clo. SW3—6A 44
Wiltshire Row. N1—1C 14
Wimbourne St. N1—2B 14
Wimpole M. W1—4F 21

Wimpole St. W1—4F to 6G 21
Winchcombe Ct. SE15—6F 63
Winchester Clo. SE17—1G 61
Winchester Sq. SE1—5B 38
Winchester St. SW1—2G 57
Winchester Wlk. SE1—5B 38
Wincott St. SE11—6D 48
Windermere Av. NW6—1A 4
Windmill Row. SE11—3C 60
Windmill St. W1—4C 22
  (in two parts)
Windmill Wlk. SE1—6D 36
Windsor Gdns. W9—3E 17
Windsor Pl. SW1—5B 46
Windsor Ter. N1—4A 14
Wine Office Ct. EC4—6D 24 & 6E 25
Winnett St. W1—2C 34
Winsland M. W2—6E 19
Winsland St. W2—6E 19
Winsley St. W1—6B 22
Winslow. SE17—3E 63
Winterton Pl. SW10—5D 54
Withers Pl. EC1—1A 26
Withington Ct. SE15—6F 63
Woburn M. WC1—2E 23
Woburn Sq. WC1—2E 23
  (in two parts)
Woburn Wlk. WC1—6E 11
Wollaston Clo. SE1—6G 49
Wolverton. SE17—2D 62 & 2E 63
Woodbridge St. EC1—1E 25
Woodchester Sq. W2—3G 17

Woodfall St. SW3—3B 56
Woodfield Gdns. W9—3D 16
Woodfield Pl. W9—3D 16
Woodfield Rd. W9—3D 16
Woodsford Sq. W14—1A 40
Woods M. W1—2C 32
Wood's Pl. SE1—4F 51
Woodstock M. W1—4F 21
Woodstock St. W1—1G 33
Wood St. EC2—6A to 4A 26
Woodville Rd. NW6—2D 4
Wooler St. SE17—3C 62
Wootton St. SE1—6D 36
Worcester Pl. EC4—3A 38
Worgan St. SE11—2A 60
Worlds End Est. SW10—6D 54
World's End Pas. SW10—6D 54
World Trade Centre. E1—3H 39
Wormwood St. EC2—5E 27
Wornington Rd. W10—3A 16
Woronzow Rd. NW8—1F 7
Worship St. EC2—2D 26
Worth Gro. SE17—3C 62
Wren St. WC1—1A 24
Wrestlers Ct. EC3—6E 27
Wrights La. W8—3G 41
Wybert St. NW1—1H 21
Wyclif St. EC1—6E 13
Wymering Mans. W9—6G 5
Wymering Rd. W9—6F 5
Wyndham M. W1—4B 20
Wyndham Pl. W1—4B 20

Wyndham St. W1—3A 20
Wyndham Yd. W1—5A 20
Wynford Rd. N1—2A 12
Wynnstay Gdns. W8—3F 41
Wynyard Ter. SE11—3B 60
Wynyatt St. EC1—5E 13
Wythburn Pl. W1—6B 20
Wyvil Rd. SW8—6F 59

Yardley St. WC1—6C 12
Yarmouth Pl. W1—6G 33
Yeoman's Row. SW3—4H 43
York Bri. NW1—1D 20
York Bldgs. WC2—4G 35
York Ga. NW1—2E 21
York Ho. Pl. W8—1H 41
York Pl. WC2—4G 35
York Rd. SE1—2A 48
Yorkshire Grey Yd. WC1—4H 23
York St. W1—4A 20
York Ter. E. NW1—2E 21
York Ter. W. NW1—2D 20
York Way. N1—1G 11
York Way Ct. N1—1H 11
Young St. W8—2H 41

Zoar St. SE1—5G 37

INDEX TO PLACES OF INTEREST, DISTRICTS, HOSPITALS, PARKS, RAILWAY AND UNDERGROUND STATIONS ETC.

Westminster R.C. Cathedral—5B 46   Wigmore Hall—6F 21   Y.M.C.A. Headquarters—5D 22
Westminster Sta.—2G 47   Working Men's College—2B 10   Y.W.C.A. Central Club—5E 23
Westminster Technical College—5C 46

GUIDE TO SELECTED PLACES OF INTEREST

BANK OF ENGLAND—1C 38
Incorporated by Royal Charter in 1694 to finance the French wars. Nationalized in 1946, the Bank of England is now the Government's bank. Its vaults contain the nation's gold reserve, it manages the National Debt, the Note issue and administers the Exchange Control Regulations. The Buildings enclose Garden Court, once the Churchyard of St Christopher-le-Stocks (a Wren Church demolished 1781), and a restored Roman mosaic (at the foot of the main staircase). Until recently a military guard protected the bank at night, a measure instigated during the Gordon Riots, 1780. Museum open.

BARBICAN—4A 26
A large area of post-war redevelopment designed to reintroduce a balanced residential and cultural life back into the heart of the business City. The precinct includes the Barbican Centre for Arts and Conferences, the London equivalent of the Lincoln Center, New York or the Centre Pompidou, Paris; facilities include: Barbican Hall, Barbican Theatre, The Pit (studio theatre), Barbican Library, Art Gallery, cinemas, restaurants, car park.

BELFAST H.M.S.—5F 39
The largest, most powerful cruiser built for the Royal Navy. Moored opposite the Tower of London, it now houses a Royal Navy museum. Admission charge.

BRITISH LIBRARY—4E 23
Created in 1973 it contains the former library departments of the British Museum and shares the same building. There are several exhibition rooms housing many items of great historical interest including Magna Carta, Lindisfarne Gospels, and Nelson's Log Books. The famous Reading Room is open to ticket-holders only. Among the notable people who have studied here are Thackeray and Karl Marx.

BRITISH MUSEUM—4E 23
The museum was founded in 1753 when the trustees were given charge of the treasures bequeathed to the nation by Sir Robert Cotton and Sir Hans Sloane. Building designed by Sir Robert Smirke and built 1823-52. Reading Room (now part of British Library) design by Sidney Smirke was added in 1857. Karl Marx being among the many to have worked there. Its unrivalled collections are comprised in the Departments of Coins and Medals, Egyptian Antiquities, Western Asiatic Antiquities, Greek and Roman Antiquities, (including the famous Elgin Marbles), British and Medieval Antiquities, Oriental Antiquities. See also Natural History Museum.

BUCKINGHAM PALACE—2H 45
London home of the Sovereign. When in residence the Royal Standard flies at the central flag pole. The Changing of the Guard normally takes place in the forecourt at 11.30. Originally built 1703 for the Duke of Buckingham, remodelled 1825 by Nash for George IV and again in 1913 by Sir A. Webb as part of the National Memorial to Queen Victoria. Not open. Adjoining are the Royal Mews and Queen's Gallery.

CABINET WAR ROOMS, Clive Steps, King Charles St.—1E 47
One of the Second World War bunkers used by Winston Chuchill and his staffs. On display are the Cabinet Office, Central Map Room, Churchill's Office and bedroom, the Transatlantic Telephone Room; all restored to their war time appearance. Admission charge.

CARNABY STREET—1A 34
Made a big noise in fashion during the late 1960's, now predominantly a Union Jack tourist attraction, pedestrianized with coloured pavement.

CHANGING OF THE GUARD
1. Buckingham Palace—2H 45. Changing of the Queen's Guard normally takes place every morning at 11.30. Alternate days in winter months. The ceremony is carried out by one of the five regiments of Foot Guards marching to the Band. Duration 30 mins. (In wet weather the Band does not accompany the Guards).
2. Horse Guards—6E 35. Changing of the Queen's Life Guard takes place in the small courtyard adjacent to Whitehall daily at 11.00 (Sundays 10.00). The ceremony is held by the two regiments of Household Cavalry, the Royal Horse Guards in Blue and the Life Guards in Red. Duration 20 mins.

COVENT GARDEN—2G 35
Since redevelopment, Covent Garden has become a lively retail trading and leisure precinct. The old market buildings restored to their original condition are now the centre of a pedestrianized area which, together with the surrounding streets, offers a wide range of small shops, restaurants etc. Adjacent are the Royal Opera House, the London Transport Museum and St Paul, Covent Garden, the actors' church. The church was designed as part of the 17th century piazza by Inigo Jones for the 4th Earl of Bedford on the site of the medieval 'Convent Garden'. A small market, given Royal Charter in 1671, it grew into London's wholesale fruit and vegetable market, since removed to Nine Elms. Admission charge to London Transport Museum.

DICKENS HOUSE—2A 24
Although the author lived here only from 1837 to 1839, 'Oliver Twist' and 'Nicholas Nickleby' were written and the 'Pickwick Papers' completed during these two years. The House is now a Museum of Dickens Memorabilia, and the headquarters of the Dickens Fellowship. Admission charge.

DISCOVERY R.R.S., St Katharine's Yacht Haven—4H 39
Polar research ship launched 1907, used by Captain Scott for Antarctic voyages. It now forms part of the Maritime Trust's Historic Ship Collection, which lies in the East Basin of St Katharine Yacht Haven.

DOCTOR JOHNSON'S HOUSE—6D 24
The famous 18th century character immortalised by Boswell, lived here from 1748 to 1759. The house contains an early edition of his Dictionary which was compiled here and published in 1755 selling for four guineas. Here also he wrote 'The Rambler' which appeared twice weekly for two years with a circulation of about five hundred. Admission charge.

DOWNING STREET—1F 47
Row of 17th cent. houses named after their builder Sir George Downing. No. 10 is the official residence of the Prime Minister; No. 11 Chancellor of the Exchequer. Not open.

GEOLOGICAL MUSEUM—5E 43
Museum of the Institute of Geological Sciences and an important research centre. Contents include a huge collection of rocks, minerals and fossils; including moon rock. New stimulating learn-and-enjoy style of exhibitions include Story of the Earth, Britain before Man, British Fossils, Gemstones and Treasures of the Earth. Admission Charge.

GUILDHALL—6B 26
Centre of the City of London's civic government for 1,000 years during the development from the ancient Court of Husting to modern Common Council. Here the 84 Livery Companies annually elect the Lord Mayor (the first Lord Mayor was elected 1192) and Sheriffs, banners of the twelve principal companies hang from the walls. Also used for municipal meetings, presentation of the freedom of the City and State Banquets. Foundations date from 1411-see The Medieval Crypt, half of which survived both Great Fire 1666 and 1940 bombs.

HORSE GUARDS—6F 35
These barracks were rebuilt in 1753. Two mounted guardsmen are on sentry duty here, and the Changing of the Guard daily at 11.00, Sundays 10.00, is a picturesque sight. Trooping the Colour, a magnificent ceremony, takes place on the Queen's official birthday on the parade ground at the rear of the building.

HOUSES OF PARLIAMENT—3G 47
Stands throughout the world as a symbol of democratic government. The Victorian Gothic building 1840-68, design by Barry and Pugin, is on the site of the Old Palace of Westminster, a royal residence from Edward the Confessor to time of Henry VIII. Being the permanent home of Parliament from 1547 the Old Palace escaped the intented destruction by Guy Fawkes, 1605, only to be destroyed by fire in 1834. Westminster Hall, the Jewel Tower, the Cloister and the Crypt survived and were incorporated into the new building. Within the Houses of Parliament the House of Lords lies to the south and the Commons to the north (rebuilt after destruction by bombing 1941) and access to both is from the Central Lobby. On the north-east corner is the Victoria Tower: the Sovereign's entrance for the State opening of Parliament. On the northside is the Clock Tower with Big Ben. The House when in session usually meets Mon. to Thurs. 14.30 onwards. Fri. 11.00. This is indicated by the Union Jack flying from Victoria Tower or a light in the Clock Tower at night. For admission to the public gallery either queue at St. Stephen's entrance or write to your M.P.

HYDE PARK—4B 32
This Royal Park covers 341 acres. On the south side from Hyde Park Corner westwards, many people take an early morning ride in Rotten Row before going to business. On Sundays the park is crowded, and it is then that the famous 'tub-thumping' public orators on rostrums and soap boxes near Mable Arch air their views to groups of listeners. The Serpentine, a large lake in the centre of the park, provides boating, and is one of London Lidos, open from the last Saturday in April until the second Sunday in October.

IMPERIAL WAR MUSEUM—4D 48
Records and illustrates all aspects of warfare, military and civil, allied and enemy, in which Britain and the Commonwealth have been involved since August 1914. Accessible to the public and to students are its unique collections of works of art, photographic and film records, and printed and manuscript material; which are contained in the extensive reference departments. Admission Charge.

KENSINGTON GARDENS—1B 42
Formerly the grounds of Kensington Palace, now a woodland park where children gather at the Round Pond to sail their boats or around the statue of Peter Pan. The Long Water should be seen from the bridge that divides it from the Serpentine.

KENSINGTON PALACE—6A 30
Originally Nottingham House, converted into a Royal Palace for William III in 1689 to designs by Wren. Interior alterations by W. Kent 1722-4. Home of Queen Victoria 1819-37 and London Museum 1951-75. Two portions are now open to the public; the 'State Apartments' and the 'Court Dress Collection'. Admission charge.

LONDON PLANETARIUM—2D 20
A vast hemispherical dome on which, by a £70,000 Zeiss projector, images of celestial bodies are shown, accurate in size, brightness and position relative to each other, also their relative paths and speeds through the night sky. Admisson charge.

LONDON TELECOM TOWER—3A 22
Built to facilitate telecommunications without interference from tall buildings.

LONDON TRANSPORT MUSEUM—2H 35
Historic vehicles and exhibits including early steam and electric locomotives, horse-buses, motor buses (including the famous 'B' type), tram cars, trolley buses, posters, tickets, signs, etc. Housed in a magnificent Victorian structure with cast iron arcades and glazed clerestories. Admission charge.

LONDON ZOO—2D 8
London Zoo opened in 1828. Now contains over 6,000 animals. Special attractions include Aquarium, Snowdon Aviary (an outdoor home for birds), Elephant and Rhinoceros Pavilion, Children's Zoo and Farm, and Nocturnal Hall where day and night are reversed. Restaurant, cafe, car park. Open every day except Christmas Day. Admission charge.

MADAME TUSSAUD'S—2D 20
Waxwork exhibition of famous and notorious characters both historical and contemporary. Tussaud's first opened in London 1802 with an exhibition of death masks from the French Revolution. Admission charge. Adjoining is the London Planetarium.

MONUMENT, THE—3D 38
Commemorates the Great Fire 1666. Designed by Wren the stone column 202ft. high is 202ft. from the origin of the fire in Pudding Lane. 311 steps to viewing platform. Admission charge.

MUSEUM OF LONDON—5H 25
One of London's modern purpose-built museums; contructed as part of the Barbican it is designed to lead visitors through the chronological development of London and environs from prehistoric times to the present day. The imaginative displays and excellent facilities earned it the Museum of the Year award 1978. Closed Mondays.

NATIONAL ARMY MUSEUM—4C 56
The history of the army from 1485 to the Falklands War 1982 (for World War I and after see Imperial War Museum).

NATIONAL GALLERY—4E 35
One of the most important picture galleries in the world, containing a representative collection of every European school of painting and works by nearly all the Great Masters.

NATIONAL PORTRAIT GALLERY—3E 35
National collection of portraits of famous British men and women dating mainly from the Tudor dynasty to the twentieth century.

NATIONAL WESTMINSTER TOWER—6E 27
At 600 ft. this is Britain's tallest solid structure.

NATURAL HISTORY MUSEUM—5E 43
Department of the British Museum, one of the world's finest natural history collections and an important research centre. As well as the traditional displays e.g. Zoology, Entomology and Palaeontology; the museum now features new stimulating visual learn-and-enjoy style exhibitions including Hall of Human Biology, Man's Place in Evolution, Introducing Ecology, Dinosaurs and Their Living Relatives, Origin of Species, British Natural History. Admission Charge.

OXFORD STREET—1C 32 to 6D 22
Shopping centre famous for its stores. Follows the line of the Roman Road west from the City. In medieval times the route for the condemned to Tyburn Gallows. Now being partly pedestrianized with the addition of trees and seats.

PICCADILLY CIRCUS—3C 34
A swirl of people, traffic and coloured lights; this is the traditional focal point of London, centering on the famous Eros statue. Both the Trocadero Centre and London Pavilion have traffic free shopping arcades and tourist attractions including the Guiness World of Records, London Experience and Rock Circus.

PUBLIC RECORD OFFICE—6C 24
Store-house for public archives, documents, State papers and National records, with public search rooms for research and study. Readers tickets on application to the Secretary. (More modern documents and facilities at Ruskin Avenue, Kew). Museum of historical items including the Domesday Book, Magna Carta, signatures and documents relating to many important people, Nelson, Wellington, Shakespeare etc. Closed Sat. & Sun.

REGENT'S PARK—1D 20
One of the largest London parks, it covers an area of 472 acres and contains the Zoo and a large boating lake. Queen Mary's Gardens are famous for roses and open-air plays.The elegant terraces surrounding the Park by John Nash are now well contrasted by two modern buildings, the Royal College of Physicians and the London Mosque.

ROYAL ACADEMY OF ARTS—4A 34
Founded by George III in 1790, the first President being Sir Joshua Reynolds. The Annual Exhibition of works by living artists is opened in the main galleries early May for a period of 12 weeks. The Private View is the first event of the London 'Season'. Gallery Shop and Framing Service.

ROYAL COURTS OF JUSTICE—1B 36
Built 1874-82 to house the Supreme Court of Judicature. Courts generally sit between 10.30-16.30 weekdays. Small exhibition of Costumes, Maces and Scrolls. Access to public galleries on both sides of the main entrance.

ROYAL EXCHANGE—1C 38
Founded 1564 by Sir T. Gresham. The original building was destroyed in the Great Fire 1666; the second in 1838. The present building by Sir W. Tate opened 1844 has a glass-roofed quadrangle; now housing the London International Financial Exchange. The gilded weather vane is in the shape of a grasshopper—the Gresham family crest.
ROYAL HOSPITAL CHELSEA—4D 56
Was designed by Sir Christopher Wren and founded in 1682 by Charles II as a home for old soldiers. The 'Chelsea Pensioner' is a well-known figure in his scarlet (Summer) or dark blue (Winter) coat. The statue of Charles II in the Figure Court is by Grinling Gibbons. In part of the spacious gardens the Flower Show is held annually by the Royal Horticultural Society.

ST JAMES'S PALACE—6B 34
Built 1532 by Henry VIII on the site of a Norman leper hospital dedicated to St. James the Less. The home of sovereigns before Buckingham Palace, now the official residence of the Prince of Wales. Foreign ambassadors are still accredited to the 'Court of St. James'. The Chapel Royal, Ambassadors' Court has been the scene of many Royal Marriages; its painted ceiling 1540 is attributed to Holbein. The Presance Chamber or Tapestry Room bears the initials of Henry VIII and Anne Boleyn. Decorations by William Morris 1881. Tudor Gatehouse facing St. James's Street H.Q. of the Gentlemen at Arms formed 1509 and Yeoman of the Guard (Beefeaters) formed 1485—together the Sovereign's dismounted bodyguard at state ceremonies. The Queen's Chapel in Marlborough Rd., designed 1623-7 by Inigo Jones was built as a Catholic Chapel for Charles I's Queen; has Royal Pews, wooden coffered ceiling and carolean panelling.

ST JAMES'S PARK—1C 46
These 93 acres were acquired by Henry VIII in 1531 to give him hunting near his Palace of Whitehall. It was under Charles II that the land was laid out by the French landscape gardener, Le Notre, to form one of the most charming of London's Royal Parks. A variety of water birds inhabit the lake, and these may be identified by labelled reproductions.

ST KATHARINE'S DOCK—4H 39
Built 1827 to designs by Thomas Telford; since 1968 redeveloped into a mixture of leisure and international trade facilities. New buildings include London World Trade Centre; historic structures have been restored ; a complex of shopping arcades and cobbled walks centre on the 200 moorings Yacht Haven.

ST PAUL'S CATHEDRAL—1G 37
Seat of the Bishopric of London and 'Parish Church of the British Commonwealth'. The present Cathedral built 1675-1710 design by Sir Christopher Wren, is on the site of the Medieval Cathedral destroyed in the Great Fire 1666. Amongst the many features are three viewing galleries, the Whispering Gallery height 100 ft., the Stone Gallery height 182 ft., and the Golden Gallery height 281 ft., also the Library, the Crypt and tombs of famous people. Admission charge to East End, Crypt and Galleries.

SCIENCE MUSEUM—4E 43
Renowned and extremely popular collection of scientific, engineering and industrial exhibits both historic and modern. Many of these can be operated by visitors. Special attention is drawn to the Children's Gallery, Aeronautical section and Wellcome Historical Medical Collection. Admission Charge.

SOUTH BANK ARTS CENTRE—5A 36
The variety of public buildings on this, the site of the 1951 Festival of Britain, illustrates the development of British architectural design between the construction of the Royal Festival Hall 1951, the Queen Elizabeth Hall, Purcell Room and Hayward Gallery 1967 and finally the National Theatre 1976. Here also are the National Film Theatre and Museum of the Moving Image.

SOUTH KENSINGTON MUSEUMS—5E 43
A whole range of museums with many exciting modern and educational displays besides being reseach centres of world importance. See Geological Museum, Natural History Museum, Science Museum, Victoria & Albert Museum.

TATE GALLERY—1F 59
The national collection of British painting, modern foreign painting and modern sculpture. Special collections of Blake, Turner, Pre-Raphaelites and Contemporary British School. Special exhibitions of great public interest are announced in the Press. Admission charge to these.

TOWER BRIDGE—5G 39
Completed in 1894; the opening of the two drawbridges to allow the passage of large ships is one of the sights of London. The Walkway (admission charge), 142 ft. above the Thames and closed in 1909, re-opened in 1982.

TOWER OF LONDON—4G 39
First built by William the Conqueror to both protect and control the City, it has been continually added to over the centuries. During its history the Tower has served as Fortress, Palace, Prison and has housed the Royal Mint, Public Records, Royal Observatory and Predecessor of the London Zoo, the Royal Menagerie. The Inner Ward is defended by a wall with thirteen towers, an inner moat; then an outer wall and outer moat. In the centre is the great Tower or Keep Called 'The White Tower'. Occupied as a Palace until the reign of James I, it was the custom for the monarch to lodge in the Tower before the coronation and ride in procession through the City to Westminster Abbey. The Crown Jewels can be seen in the Jewel House and include the Crown of Queen Elizabeth (consort of George VI) set with the 'Koh-i-Nor' diamond. A brass plate on Tower Green marks the site of the scaffold. The Ceremony of the Keys is enacted nightly at 22.00 when the main gate is locked. Admission charge, extra charges to Crown Jewels and Regimental Museum. Jewel House closed February.

TRAFALGAR SQUARE—4E 35
Laid out as a war memorial and named after the victory of Trafalgar, the square was completed in 1841. in the centre rises Nelson's Column. 170 ft. high overall, allowing Nelson a view of the sea. The lions at the base are by Landseer. Fountains and pigeons delight onlookers. Facing Whitehall is a 17th-century equestrian statue of Charles I, the Martyr King.

VICTORIA AND ALBERT MUSEUM—5F 43
One of the great world museums of fine and applied art, it illustrates artistic achievement throughout the centuries and is arranged into two groups. (a) Primary Collections—of style, period or nationality. (b) Departmental Collections—sculpture, textiles, woodwork, etc. The museum incorporates the National Art Library. Admission Charge.

WESTMINSTER ABBEY—3F 47
Collegiate church of St. Peter in Westminster, under jurisdiction of Dean and Chapter; subject only to the Sovereign. All English Sovereigns from William I to Elizabeth II have been crowned here except Edward V and VIII. Founded by Edward the Confessor on site of earlier building 1065. Rebuilt in Edward's honour by Henry III in French Gothic style, architect Henry of Rheims and rededicated 1269. Amongst the many features are the Shrine of Edward the Confessor, Coronation Chair, Henry VII Chapel, Royal Tombs and Monuments, Poets Corner, Grave of the Unknown Warrior, Chapter House, Museum of Treasures, Chapel of the Pyx. Admission charge to Royal Chapels, Poets Corner, Museum, Chapter House.

WESTMINSTER CATHEDRAL—5B 46
Roman Catholic Cathedral, seat of the Cardinal Archbishop of Westminster. Built 1895-1903, J.F. Bentley in Early Christian Byzantine style. The exterior of alternate brick and stone bands is beautifully offset by modern architecture and piazza linking with Victoria Street. Square Campanile, St. Edward's Tower is 284 ft. high, lift to viewing gallery. Admission charge to Campanile.

WHITEHALL—5F 35
Broad processional way between Trafalgar and Parliament Squares lined by Government Offices and Departments. Name derives from Whitehall Palace destroyed by fire 1678 (except for the Banqueting House). Other buildings include the Old Admiralty, Horse Guards, Dover House. The many statues and monuments include the Cenotaph.

SHOPPING CENTRES

Not to Scale

WEST END

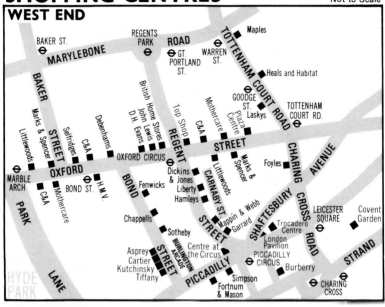

BAKER ST.

REGENTS PARK

ROAD

Maples

MARYLEBONE

GT. PORTLAND ST.

WARREN ST.

TOTTENHAM COURT ROAD

Heals and Habitat

BAKER

British Home Stores

John Lewis

D.H. Evans

GOODGE ST.

Laskys

TOTTENHAM COURT RD.

Marks & Spencer

Debenhams

Top Shop

Mothercare

Plaza Centre

Littlewoods

STREET

Selfridges

C&A

REGENT

C&A

STREET

Marks & Spencer

Foyles

CHARING

AVENUE

OXFORD CIRCUS

Dickins & Jones

Littlewoods

MARBLE ARCH

OXFORD

Fenwicks

Liberty

BOND

CARNABY ST.

CROSS

LEICESTER SQUARE

Covent Garden

C&A

Mothercare

BOND ST.

H.M.V.

Hamleys

Mappin & Webb

Garrard

SHAFTESBURY

ROAD

Trocadero Centre

PARK

Chappells

Sotheby

STREET

London Pavilion

STRAND

Asprey

Cartier

Kutchinsky

Tiffany

BURLINGTON ARCADE

STREET

Centre at the Circus

PICCADILLY CIRCUS

Burberry

HYDE PARK

LANE

PICCADILLY

Simpson

Fortnum & Mason

CHARING CROSS

KENSINGTON HIGH STREET

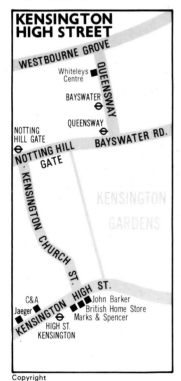

WESTBOURNE GROVE

Whiteleys Centre

QUEENSWAY

BAYSWATER

QUEENSWAY

NOTTING HILL GATE

BAYSWATER RD.

NOTTING HILL GATE

KENSINGTON

KENSINGTON GARDENS

KENSINGTON CHURCH ST.

HIGH ST.

C&A

John Barker

Jaeger

British Home Store

Marks & Spencer

KENSINGTON HIGH ST.

HIGH ST. KENSINGTON

KNIGHTSBRIDGE

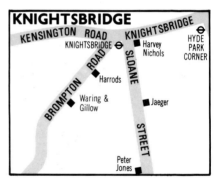

KENSINGTON ROAD

KNIGHTSBRIDGE

KNIGHTSBRIDGE

Harvey Nichols

HYDE PARK CORNER

ROAD

SLOANE

BROMPTON

Harrods

Waring & Gillow

Jaeger

STREET

Peter Jones

VICTORIA

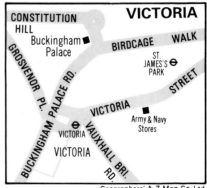

CONSTITUTION HILL

Buckingham Palace

BIRDCAGE WALK

ST. JAMES'S PARK

GROSVENOR PL.

STREET

VICTORIA

Army & Navy Stores

BUCKINGHAM PALACE RD.

VICTORIA

VAUXHALL BRI. RD.

VICTORIA

Geographers' A-Z Map Co. Ltd.

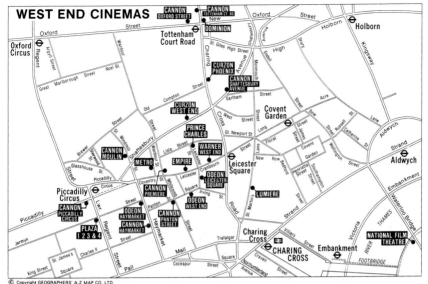

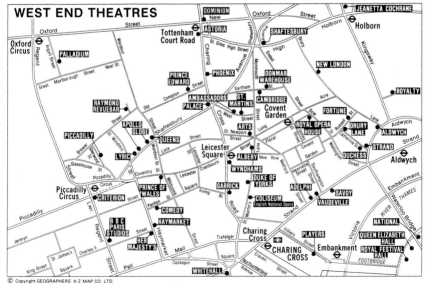

Printed and bound in Great Britain by BPCC Hazell Books Ltd
Member of BPCC Ltd, Aylesbury, Bucks, England